EST MARATHON '97
The One-Act Plays

SMITH AND KRAUS PUBLISHERS
Contemporary Playwrights / Collections

Act One Festival '95
Act One Festival '95

EST Marathon '94: The One-Act Plays
EST Marathon '95: The One-Act Plays
EST Marathon '96: The One-Act Plays
EST Marathon '97: The One-Act Plays

Humana Festival: 20 One-Acts Plays 1976–1996
Humana Festival '93: The Complete Plays
Humana Festival '94: The Complete Plays
Humana Festival '95: The Complete Plays
Humana Festival '96: The Complete Plays
Humana Festival '97: The Complete Plays
Humana Festival '98: The Complete Plays

Women Playwrights: The Best Plays of 1992
Women Playwrights: The Best Plays of 1993
Women Playwrights: The Best Plays of 1994
Women Playwrights: The Best Plays of 1995
Women Playwrights: The Best Plays of 1996
Women Playwrights: The Best Plays of 1997

EST MARATHON '97
The One-Act Plays

CONTEMPORARY PLAYWRIGHTS
SERIES

SK
A Smith and Kraus Book

812.041
E79
1997

A Smith and Kraus Book
Published by Smith and Kraus, Inc.
PO Box 127, Lyme, NH 03768

Copyright ©1998 by Smith and Kraus
All rights reserved
Manufactured in the United States of America
Cover and Text Design by Julia Hill

First Edition: July 1998
10 9 8 7 6 5 4 3 2 1

The Library of Congress Cataloging-In-Publication Data

EST Marathon '97: the one-act plays / edited by Marisa Smith. —1st ed.
    p.   cm.   —(Contemporary playwrights series) ISSN 1067-9510
    ISBN 1-57525-135-3

    1. One-act plays, American. 2. American drama—20th century. 3. Ensemble Studio Theater.
I. Smith, Marisa. II. Series.

    PS627.053E88   1995
    812'.04108—dc20

                  95-2287
                  CIP

CONTENTS

Mafia on Prozac

BY EDWARD ALLAN BAKER

THIS PLAY IS DEDICATED TO JACK CAPUTO.

THE AUTHOR

Plays, produced Off-Broadway and Off-Off Broadway, include *A Public Street Marriage, Prairie Avenue, North of Providence, Dolores, Lady of Fadima, The Buffer, Face Divided, Rosemary with Ginger, Mafia on Prozac, The Bride of Olneyville Square, In the Spirit,* and *A Deadmans Apartment.*

Plays published include *North of Providence, Dolores, Lady of Fadima, Rosemary with Ginger, Face Divided, A Deadmans Apartment* (Dramatists Play Service.) *Dolores* is also published in Best Short Plays 1988–89 by Applause Theater Books.

Screenplays include *Dolores* (award-winning short film directed and produced by Ed Bianchi and shot by Gordon Willis that starred Judith Ivey and Laura Innes), *Prairie Avenue* (from the full-length play that starred Ed Harris and Amy Madigan in L.A. and was one of ten screenplays selected for further development at Sundance in 1990), *One Track Mind, Dolmes* (full-length screenplay), *The Buffer,* and *WelcomeTaBrooklyn,* (all for Stella Pictures), *Rosemary with Ginger* (for ShowTime), and co-writer for *A Deadly Secret* (HBO).

Baker is currently Adjunct Professor of Playwriting at Sarah Lawrence College in Bronxville, NY, head writer of Radio Drama(s) for "Down Eerie Street" Productions (Jack Douglas, Producer), and two new plays, *No Water, No Ice* and *The Settlement* are in development at the Ensemble Studio Theater in New York City.

ORIGINAL PRODUCTION

Mafia on Prozac was originally produced at the Ensemble Studio Theatre's Marathon '97. It was directed by Ron Stetson, lighting by Greg MacPherson, sets by Bruce Goodrich, costumes by Laura Churba, with the following cast:

TEE	Victor Slezak
JAY	Michael McCormick
MATT	Joe White

AUTHOR'S NOTE

Mafia on Prozac was my eighth play in the EST One-Act Marathon and the only thing that transcends my pride in that accomplishment is being a *member* of the Ensemble Studio Theatre. I love it in the way I loved my Uncle Richie, a poor man who never went anywhere, but was always there (for me) by "being in the moment" and giving me nothing but confidence, a Pall Mall, and a good feeling about my/our family. Every person should have an Uncle Richie. Every playwright should have an Ensemble Studio Theatre.

CHARACTERS
JAY
TEE
MATT

PLACE
A pier in Jerusalem, Rhode Island

TIME
Midnight in mid-summer

SETTING
A wooden dock that's been through many a hurricane. Water is always heard lapping its legs. A buoy-bell is heard off in the distance. And there is moonlight. Two lawn chairs are on the dock in the pre-set. Small TV-table has a thermos of coffee and two demitasse cups atop it. A lemon and a knife, too. At the foot of the stage-right lawn chair is a cassette player. All is calm. Like nature on Prozac. Pre-show music is dominated by Mario Lanza music.

Pre-show lights fade to Black with the pre-show music (a specific Lanza tune) now coming from the cassette player on the dock then: Lights up on Jay and Tee, both 50ish, sipping coffee, slowly, and gazing out to the ocean. Close to the edge of the dock is a sack with a man inside. He is very still. In the stage-right lawn chair is Tee. Thin. Nicely dressed. Obviously has a tailor. In the stage-left chair is Jay. Little on the heavy side. Clothes are baggy. He sports a black beret. Tee finishes his coffee. Punches off the music. Looks to Jay.

TEE: Music do anythin to your Italian heart?

JAY: I hate to admit it...

TEE: Nothin, right?

JAY: Used to give me a hard-on. Brought me tears.

TEE: Made me proud a my blood but now...

JAY: Nothin. Not even a twinge.

TEE: So what the fuck is going on? *(Beat.)* Do you do this anymore? *(Tee bites the side of his hand.)*

JAY: Been months. Months.

TEE: How 'bout this? *(He places the tops of his fingers under his chin and flicks outward.)*

JAY: Last time was probly last year at this time.

TEE: While drivin down Chalkstone, when was the last time you went "ooh-dee-fah, what an ass?"

JAY: Last time was probly last year at this time.

TEE: Never do it anymore.

JAY: Never do it anymore.

TEE: So what is it? What the fuck is goin on?

(Brief pause then suddenly a voice screams out from inside the potato sack.)

MATT: CAN WE GET ON WITH IT?! CAN ONE OF YOU JUST ROLL ME OFF INTO THE DEEP?! MY LIFE IS PASSING BEFORE MY EYES AND I WANT IT TO STOP! SO HOW 'BOUT IT GENTS?! ONE-TWO-THREE AND SPLASH!

TEE: What's your fucken hurry?

JAY: We're givin you time.

MATT: I'm definitely going to die, correct?

TEE: Without a doubt.

MATT: Then do it!

TEE: Fuck you an shut up or we'll make you live til the sun comes up! We'll do it when we do it!

(Silence for a moment then softly.)

MATT: Please kill me…please kill me…please kill me…

JAY: Fucken pa-ta-da head.

TEE: *(To Jay.)* He wanted to screw around.

JAY: *(To Matt.)* We're the consequences.

TEE: *(To Jay.)* So if he wants to die tell 'im to keep his trap shut.

JAY: *(To Matt.)* We're talkin here.

(Matt pops his head out of the sack for the first time.)

MATT: Can't you roll me over then do your talkin? *(He takes a beat to look out at the water. Little bit of fear crosses his boyish thirty-five year old face.)*

JAY: Twenty years…

TEE: An change. Twenty an change.

JAY: Twenty an change we been doin this an never ever talk or meet afta a job.

TEE: Never afta. Rules of the State.

JAY: Only talk before.

MATT: Can I be allowed to say WHAT THE FUCK ARE YOU TWO TALKIN ABOUT?! WHAT STATE?!

JAY: You haven't been listenin for the last hour on uz talkin here?

MATT: What the fuck else am I gonna do?! Fish?!

JAY: Think what we been talkin about is nothin?

MATT: Of all the fucken hit-men in Providence I end up with Abbott and Costello! Jesus!

JAY: You didn't learn anythin?

MATT: No No sorry, the "I need to learn somethin" door shut as soon as you rolled me down this dock. With death this close—be like tryin to get an erection. What's the point?

JAY: *(Looks to Tee.)* Speakin of which…

TEE: *(Softly.)* Erection.

JAY: Wear your a-lastic-pecka-ring last night?

TEE: Tee. *(Beat.)* Still got it on.

JAY: What? The Doctor says the a-lastic-pecka-ring is only for when we're sleepin.

MATT: See?! This is what I'm gettin at!

TEE: *(To Jay.)* There was no movement. No enlargement. No breaking. So I kept it on.

JAY: You gotta be patient about it.

TEE: I know. I know. Stress doesn't help things.

JAY: Fucken stress destroys desire.

TEE: Every time.

JAY: Mary takin it okay?

TEE: What?

JAY: The a-lastic-pecka-ring.

TEE: She don't see it. How 'bout Bett? She see it?

JAY: She wanted to. I showed her. No big deal.

MATT: Oh god oh god oh god, if this is Limbo, HELL must be un-fucken-believable! *(He retreats back into the sack.)*

JAY: *(To Tee.)* Lately, me an Bett been sharin more. Talkin, yunno? I figured somethin out that has made bein with her okay, an that's when I'm with her I think an try to believe that it's our last time together.

TEE: Then you're not thinkin a things you can't give her.

JAY: Exactly! That's why you're my reflection you crafty sonofabitch, I love ya ya bastard cause you know, you just know you mother-fucka you do it to me all the time, honest ta shit you kill me ya cocksucka, you... *(Matt's head pops out of the sack.)*

MATT: ALL RIGHT! I THINK HE GETS IT!

TEE: *(Stands, goes to Matt.)* You know pa-ta-da head, you're inchin your way back to life.

JAY: *(Stands next to Tee.)* Oh man in the sack.

TEE: You're here with us cause you couldn't keep your Mista O'Malley away from a seventeen year old an—

MATT: I fell in love with her!

JAY: *(To Matt.)* Let 'im finish, ssh, let 'im finish.

TEE: Now you got a wife an a boy, right?

MATT: You know I do.

TEE: An the boy was seein Miss Nero, correct?

MATT: Yeah-yeah-yeah...

TEE: Then what? You take one look at that HUGE ass she's got an go fucken ga-ga?! She weighs what? Two, two-fifty?

JAY: Tee. Wrong daughter. You're thinkin a Tina.

MATT: Not Tina. It's Nina.

JAY: *(To Tee.)* Nina. The younger one.

TEE: Tina's the older one?

JAY: Nineteen. Twenty. Gigantic ass.

TEE: An Nina is...

JAY: Sixteen. Seventeen.

MATT: Seventeen.

TEE: Seventeen.

MATT: Seventeen.

TEE: Wow! *(Goes to kick Matt but stops short.)* Fucken WOW is all I can say.

MATT: I fell in love with her. First time I saw her I couldn't stop from...uh...
  (Beat.)
JAY: Keep goin pa-ta-da head..."couldn't stop from...?"
MATT: Whenever I saw her I...I cried...
  (Jay and Tee laugh.)
MATT: I'm serious! I couldn't stop it. If she said "lets run away" an say I had a million bucks not to run away, I'd run away.
(More laughter.)
MATT: Her face made my past an present disappear and...that included my son. I couldn't see past her beauty an our future together. When I smelled her or or saw her—my son meant nothin.
TEE: You pathetic piece a shit.
MATT: I know, I know...but I...I never felt that strong for anyone before her so I went with it.
TEE: You did all that knowin she was a Nero?
MATT: I knew she was a Nero.
TEE: An it didn't fucken connect—"Oh Christ, I'm feelin the firm breasts of a MINOR who happens to be the daughter of a powerful State Senator?!" Daughter of State Senator Nero, a powerful man in our world as well as your world!
MATT: I didn't feel her firm breasts! I mean I knew they were firm but I honored her request to...uh...to not hunger for her, to not make her afraid, so we kissed, lightly, at first.
JAY: Held hands.
TEE: Whispered.
MATT: Whispered, yup-yup, held hands.
JAY: An your wife?
MATT: She's in the routine, yunno, same shit as everybody. Watch TV until we die, yunno, an an desire is somethin that's a combination of fear an politeness an you inch up, inch back, inch up...
JAY: She's there.
TEE: Not there.
JAY: There.
TEE: Not there.
MATT: That's right an when she's there oh god the plannin an the timin, an when she's not there well combine the pain of that with visual stimuli and...
TEE: Ay, fuck all that, all right?! Hearin this shit ain't gonna make you die any

sooner so the bottom line the way I see it is this—you got a hard-on for your son's girlfriend who just so happens to be a Nero, then—

JAY: *(Cuts him off.)* Hey hey hey this has real shades of "Death In Venice." Rememba the one book we had in the Pen? Tee? Rememba?

TEE: You read it to me for two years. 'Bout the Old Homo.

JAY: *(Recites.)* "I was like the gamecock that lets his wings droop in the battle. That must be the Love-God himself, that makes us hang our heads at sight of beauty and weighs our proud spirits low as the ground."

MATT: This isn't happening, please please just push me off the side...

JAY: *(To Matt.)* You're the gamecock with the drooping wings.

TEE: Don't put "droop" and "gamecock" in the same sentence, capice?

JAY: Oh shit, right right, sorry. *(Pause. Jay thinks aloud.)* So the man-in-the-sack avoids his wife an son to go afta Nina The Goddess—ignorin the fact she's a Nero an...

TEE: *(Cuts him off.)* Fuck him. Jay. Fuck him. We got things to act on. He's a nobody to us. Fuck him. That is a rule of the State. Nobody serves the State who's a nobody. Whose happiness is he pursuing? Huh? His own. Selfish prick. Fuck him. Didn't you hear him earlier when he blamed "visual stimuli" or some such shit?! He's turnin it around! That's not service to the State! He got a hard-on and the hearts for innocence and a young firm body then—

JAY: Lost his sense of reality.

TEE: That's all the fuck it is.

JAY: An now—

TEE: An now the rules-of-the-State apply.

(They stare at the man-in-the-sack.)

TEE: That's it.

(They stare a bit longer then—approach slowly the man-in-the-sack. A decision has been made. They bend to do their job when Jay has a sudden thought—he straightens up.)

JAY: Is it possible, and it's soundin more an more like it might be, that he fucked up without bein to blame for fuckin up, you understand me? That he fell flat on his pa-ta-da face because of—CHANCE. And that Tee can't be helped.

TEE: Yeah sure IF what you're sayin, happened.

MATT: I just want to die! I honest to god want to die!

JAY: Hear me, Tee. Most people think stuff happens to them because of CHOICE but I once heard that CHANCE happens to us more than CHOICE.

TEE: So whaddaya sayin? That we hafta decide whether this idiot was hit by chance or choice? Is that what your fucken brain is cookin up for me to buy? That chance made his dick go up an ours go down?

JAY: He said he cried when he first saw her.

TEE: That's true.

JAY: He said he lost sight of his son.

TEE: Totally.

JAY: And his wife.

TEE: Psst. Gone.

JAY: He quelled his hunger at Miss Nero's request. He ignored the consequences.

TEE: He did. Without thinkin. He just did it.

JAY: Tee…we hafta think this one through. Tee…I think—we're bein tested. *(Jay sits in his lawn chair. Tee takes a moment. Looks at Jay. Then sits.)*

TEE: Tested? By who?

JAY: Uh you're…well you're not gonna believe this but um… *(Beat.)* Well for the past six months I I haven't said anythin to you about it but I uh… *(Beat.)* Um in my dreams I uh talk with…Al Capone. *(Matt bangs his head on the dock a few times in disbelief. Tee takes a long moment to stare at Jay, then:)*

TEE: Did you happen to see what I got your daughter for her College graduation?

JAY: He told me I had to undo everythin. To make the Mafia of the State disappear. Like the Mayans. No trace. No more movies.

TEE: It was a scarf.

JAY: Tee. Al Capone came to me.

TEE: I want to cry but I can't. I should have a sick feelin in my stomach but I don't. My best friend an partner is goin against everythin we lived for all these years an I'm…

JAY: Tee, wait…

TEE: An it does nothin but threaten the very states we have formed because that's the only way we can live without killin one another an an you wanna believe chance struck fuckhead here an it's a sign that Al Capone is givin us a test THEN we're supposed to undo FUCKEN UNDO the very organization that's given us a sense of purpose because in a way we serve justice for those, like fuckhead here, who fall through the cracks of the State an an never in all our jobs, never once did CHANCE become an issue til fucken now an I want to know WHAT IS GOIN ON?!

WHY FOR THE PAST SIX MONTHS HAVE I BEEN FEELIN BARE ASS, FUCKEN BARE ASS NAKED?!

(Pause. Tee and Jay stare out at the water.)

TEE: Lookit the light of the moon goin up an down in the waves.

JAY: First time in twenty years I noticed the waves.

(Buoy bell heard off in the distance.)

MATT: So, just to break this up fella's, for a sec…

JAY: So man in the sack, you might just walk away because of chance.

MATT: NOOOO! What is it with you two fucken idiots?! Lay a little too much cement?! Jesus fucken Christ, I went afta Nina Nero because I hated my life an was lookin for some danger an then one day THERE IT WAS in my living room in front of my wedding pictures! I saw Nina an tears rolled down my face. I said, "hello, I'm…peelin onions." She smiled. And in that moment, IN THAT FUCKEN MOMENT, I saw her and I havin a future! Her curled up by my side as we jeeped through Haiti. Eating breakfast in bed. Picking flowers. Reading Steven King. Aloud. Watching painters paint. Fishermen fish. Weavers weave. Never bein more than an arms length away except when absolutely necessary. I I saw all this in that moment in my living room in front of my wedding pictures. Am I supposed to ignore all that? An an then just before you two clowns kidnapped me in the Dunkin Donuts parkin lot, I was feelin very guilty for my familys future…My son the target of ridicule at his school for Teens With Special Needs. T-W-S-N. But then Nina's face and black stallion hair would appear before me, her eyes like two black olives in the white snow an I I would start to cry an…

JAY: "Jeeped through Haiti?!"

TEE: JAY! Snap out of it! Forget him! All right?! It's this CAPONE thing that has me worried inside deep! We known each other for a thousand years an together we done a million things like rollin fuckheads like him down this wooden dock in all kinds of weather, me an you, side by side, doin what we do an doin it right. Good soldiers. The "quiet assassins" they call us in social clubs an Bocce courts, but lately…lately an I don't know if it's coffee we been havin with Rita every mornin or what but we been suffering an we been sufferin cause things don't apply no more an…

MATT: *(Sarcastically.)* Oh yeah, it's the coffee…

TEE: Shut up!

JAY: Look at me, Tee…Capone is undoing OUR habits before we undo the habits of the State.

TEE: Capone. The most famous mob-boss that side a Providence appears to you as an angel an you're buyin it?! Then I suppose you're goin to want my help in tellin this to Nero?!

MATT: Love to be around for that one.

JAY: Exactly! That's why you're my reflection you crafty sonofabitch, I love ya ya bastard cause you know, you just know you mother-fucka you do it to me all the time honest ta shit you kill me you cocksucka...

TEE: I don't know anythin! You hear me?' I know nothin!

JAY: "That night he had a fearful dream—if dream be the right word for a mental and physical experience which indeed befall him in deep sleep..."

TEE: I hate that fucken book.

JAY: "As a thing quite apart and real to his senses yet without his seeing himself as present in it."

TEE: I have dreams, right, of maybe Sophia Loren but I'm not runnin around an an uh slippin gowns off of the shoulders of every Broad I see!

JAY: What?

MATT: He just made a bad attempt at comparing his havin dreams to your Capone visitation.

JAY: Tee, we know each other all our lives an we existed together cause we passed on the things that would part us. We overlooked stuff about the other an kept on the things that welded us as one cause we knew somewhere deep that's what was important, you see where I'm goin with this?

TEE: Not a fucken clue.

MATT: He's sayin you remain friends because each other's short-comings are overlooked because together you have a larger purpose that goes without saying.

TEE: What the fuck in me do you overlook? Tell me. I mean I overlook your fruity-notions 'bout life, an that fruity hat you wear an...

JAY: *(Cuts him off.)* You're a selfish asshole.

MATT: Uh before this goes any further...

TEE: *(To Jay.)* An asshole.

MATT: No. He said "a selfish asshole."

TEE: That's what you overlooked all these years?

JAY: Every time we're together.

TEE: Every time we're together.

JAY: Yup. You carry that chip-on-your-shoulder. Pissed inside about something really big that won't come out. Always got up my ass that you have this attitude about people—that you're more special than them.

TEE: Anythin else while you're at it?

JAY: Listen. No big deal. I overlooked it. Successfully. We had to work. We got families. I had to put Rita through college. Much more important than worrying 'bout you bein a selfish asshole—

(Tee turns away from Jay. Hurt.)

JAY: But I should add here that Rita adores you as her Godfather an said to me just the other day that her havin breakfast with me an you this past year was really special.

(Tee doesn't look at Jay. Pause.)

MATT: What's your daughter plannin on doin out in the world afta college?

JAY: Gonna be a Pharmacist.

(Beat. Jay rises from his lawn chair. Removes his wallet. Tee is still looking away. Jay bends to Matt to show him a photo of Rita.)

MATT: Oh nice. You should be proud.

(Tee bursts up from his chair.)

TEE: I don't fucken believe this!

JAY: Hey you asked!

TEE: You should've lied!

JAY: I don't lie!

MATT: Excuse me?

JAY: An you know I don't lie!

TEE: I OVERLOOKED it!

JAY: Okay, okay, lets just calm…

TEE: *(Cuts him off.)* This news breaks me up.

JAY: Well that shit-a-yours on my "fruity notions" doesn't exactly sit well with me!

TEE: Fruity notions versus selfish asshole?!

MATT: The asshole wins.

TEE: Thank you.

MATT: Now that I'm in can I make a suggestion here? You two obviously have much to talk on, so roll me over an then…

TEE: You're an idiot!

MATT: You're an asshole!

(Tee straddles the man-in-the-sack.)

TEE: I got a good mind to bring your wife an kid here, whaddaya think a that, smart ass?!

MATT: Oh take it out on me cause your best friend for years has been hidin the fact he thinks you're a selfish asshole!

TEE: Yeah I bet they'd love to talk to you for a while 'fore droppin you off a the side a this dock!

JAY: Or we let you go back an have your kid kick the shit out of you while Nero watches. *(Beat.)* You know, I'm goin to suggest that to Nero... when he gets here.

TEE AND MATT: WHAT?!

TEE: Nero is comin here?! To the dock?!

MATT: I don't want to see him!

JAY: You might not.

TEE: You arranged this an didn't tell me?!

MATT: Oh kill me! Kill me!

TEE: *(Stays on Jay.)* Knowin that he's comin you still brought up the idea of lettin pa-ta-da head walk?! Do you know how Nero will take that?!

JAY: I asked him to come because that's when I hit him with Capone's message. Listen to me, Tee...it'll prove it really happened if my action supports my dream.

TEE: A fruity notion! There it is. There it is. Another one of your...

JAY: *(Cuts him off, firmly.)* I SWEAR ON MY DAUGHTER'S FUTURE I BEEN TALKIN WITH AL CAPONE!

(Tee stares at Jay in stunned disbelief. Jay turns away.)

JAY: He an me talked on everything...We even talked about movies an he told me he likes the Godfather ones the best, not crazy 'bout the last one.

MATT: Weak storyline. Bad idea dragging the Vatican into it.

JAY: Without Pacino it's nothin.

MATT: Well, no shit.

TEE: Hey-hey-hey-HEY! First you're talkin to Capone about the movies an now you're talkin movies with the man-in-the-sack?! *(Beat.)* An while we're on it, I happen to like the last one the best!

MATT: I give it a Cee.

TEE: I give it an A-FUCKEN-PLUS!

JAY: I'm gonna give it a c-plus.

MATT: GOODFELLA'S...A-plus all the way.

JAY: Capone said no more mob movies shoulda been made afta that one.

MATT: Well then Capone knows his movies.

TEE: SHUT UP! BOTH OF YOU SHUT THE FUCK UP!

MATT: *(After a beat.)* Listen up there, KILL ME, then forget this night and return to your life as you have always known it!

JAY: That's over, Tee. That's what I'm tryin to tell ya. No more life as you have known it, as WE have known it.

MATT: Don't listen to that crap!

TEE: *(To Jay.)* If I don't follow along?

JAY: I'm afraid you an I—

TEE: Will be no more.

JAY: It'd hafta be that way. *(Jay sits.)*

TEE: A course. A course. *(Tee sits. Beat.)* So I either go along with this Capone thing an we live or die through it or—

JAY: You kill him. Go your way. I go mine. An maybe, just maybe, I'll be escorted down this dock by you an your new partner an you'll be supportin the current State just like always while I... *(Getting emotional.)* While I tried for change because I took a message from my dreams an an stuff...the everyday shit, just got unimportant includin below my belt which used to count more than breath itself...

MATT: Oh god he's going to get to the book! He's thinkin up somethin from the book! *(Matt lowers his head into the sack.)*

JAY: "Now daily the naked God with cheeks aflame drove his four fire-breathing steeds through heaven's spaces."

TEE: And if I'm wrong, you won't be rollin me down this dock?

JAY: There will be new rules because the State will have changed.

TEE: To what? What do our people do in you an Capone's new State? What the fuck you goin to tell Nero?

JAY: *(Beat.)* Latin Kings.

TEE: Latin Kings.

JAY: They're younger. Fiercer. There's more of 'em every day. They're in politics now. They're cops. Crossing guards. Judges. So it's now time for us to blend in with pa-ta-da heads people. Leave no trace. *(Steps closer to Tee.)* It's like us joinin the Witness Protection Program, but NOT joinin the Witness Protection Program.

(Tee stays fixed on Jay. Then:)

TEE: Hey turtle, da-cipher for me, will ya?

MATT: He's sayin your State is defeated. An the new army is in place. Stronger. He's sayin your only escape is to go legit in my World but listen man, if I don't want to return there WHY THE FUCK WOULD YOU WANT TO SPEND YOUR REMAININ DAYS THERE?! IT MAKES NO SENSE!

TEE: That's a good point.

JAY: Fuck him. He's just a coward. Cowards have no good points.

MATT: Why would you want to live with people whose masks are skin deep?! I mean the world you're thinkin of escapin to has an underbelly of rage and perversion that will drive you mad! It will eat away at you! And the boredom! The fucken boredom made solid by boring people with troubled kids! And fucken virtue is reduced to not parking in a handicapped space! That's it! I know cause I fell into it an then sought danger, thank god, and here I am, happily I guess, a-man-in-a-sack—NOW DO THE JOB! FINISH THE JOB!

TEE: Chance my ass. *(Tee walks away from Jay and Matt.)*

JAY: It's chance, Tee. No man would screw his son like he did by choice.

TEE: He's a horny little bastard an wanted danger who hurt his god-damn wife.

MATT: It crushed her.

JAY: She's part of his chance. You see, her life is about to improve. An an his kid, well, he's a kid an when he's forty he'll look back without bein able to help it an his memory will either destroy him or he'll fix what he can. And move on.

MATT: Shiiit!

JAY: It happened to me an you, Tee, with our fathers. We hit forty an memories came up but by then—they were dyin an wanted to forget what we wanted them to tell uz, rememba? *(Beat.)* I was at my old man's feet all knotted up inside an wantin him to take me into his workin-class arms to hold me an to whisper "I'm proud a you more than you'll ever know an…an don't ever doubt the love I got in my heart for you cause you're my boy, my son." *(Beat.)* An your Pop, Tee, was rolled off this dock by Izzo and Spiridi, his stomach held more cancer than food, and what did he say to you the day before?

TEE: *(Softly.)* Stavita e come una fosca per bambino breve e pieno di merda.

JAY: "Life is like a baby's diaper, short and shitty."

TEE: So whaddaya gettin at, Jay? That I gotta go to the Pen an cry with my three boys?

MATT: You got three sons in jail?!

JAY: *(To Tee.)* I'm sayin fuckhead here should get up an return to his family an fix things AND we should let him AND we should check up on him every week makin sure he's doin it.

MATT: I'M NOT GOIN TO DO THAT! Do you hear me?! I can't do that kind of stuff! I can't be open like that! I'd rather die than face off with my kid or my wife!

JAY: You'd rather die than talk it out with your family?!

MATT: Yes! I have no explanation for it…it's just that way so spare me from life, please!

JAY: You'd rather die than talk it out with…

TEE: Jay! Why is that so hard for you to undastand?

(Jay turns to Tee.)

JAY: YOU'D rather die than talk it out with YOUR family?!

TEE: Some people can't talk on stuff so close with those who are close.

JAY: You'd rather die than talk it...

MATT: ANSWER HIM!

TEE: *(To Jay.)* I...I don't know.

JAY: You been talkin to me all these years, openly.

TEE: Not really talkin. Just goin along. I say what it takes an...

JAY: What the fuck does that mean?

TEE: I never told you everythin, okay, that's all, cause I couldn't. Can't. An when you started tryin to get me to open up more, what did I do?

JAY: I don't rememba...

MATT: YOU REMEMBER A WHOLE FUCKEN BOOK WORD-FOR-WORD AN YOU CAN'T REMEMBER THE ONE TIME HE...

TEE: *(Ignores Matt.)* I backed off.

JAY: Yeah. So what? You backed off. I was used to it.

MATT: Yeah you just thought he was a selfish asshole.

TEE: That true?

JAY: What the fuck

TEE: Yeah what the fuck—

MATT: What the fuck—

JAY: *(After a beat.)* But—you'd rather die than talk it out with your family?

TEE: My family's a fucken mess! I don't hafta to tell you, you know. I got three fucken maniacs for sons an I take the blame every fucken mother-fucken day for lettin that happen. I got lazy an thought they could do it, yunno, live life on their own but I failed. I I just look at my family to see what a failure I am...

JAY: Whaddaya tellin me here, Jay?

MATT: He's tellin you he's not a selfish asshole like you've been thinkin all these years an he's sayin the chip-on-his-shoulder is about failure and regret.

TEE: Shame.

MATT: Failure, shame, and regret.

TEE: I shoulda done more.

MATT: I can relate.

TEE: I shoulda shown 'em how to grow a tomata. How to put down a cement patio. Get 'em into a ceramics class or somethin. It's like they went from bein fourteen to twenty-one in a blink.

MATT: Well at least you had three shots at it. I mean I got only the one son an often felt if I had another kid I'd learn from my mistakes an...

JAY: He has triplets.

MATT: Triplets?! In jail?!

JAY: Only ones in the whole penal system.

MATT: You know I gotta say somethin here an that's this: the triplets in jail just convinced me that YES YOU ARE TRYING TO DRIVE ME MAD! NERO IS BEHIND THIS BRAND OF TORTURE, ISN'T HE?!

JAY: *(Ignores Matt.)* Tee...

MATT: YOU TWO ARE THE PRICE FOR LOVIN HIS DAUGHTER!

(Tee bursts from his chair. Stands over Matt.)

TEE: FUCK YOU! I'M SICK OF YOU NOW! "...price for lovin his daughter?!?" No shithead! This is about the price for NOT lovin your son! How old's the kid?!

MATT: He's sixteen but we're goin to get into this now?

TEE: I need to make up my mind one way or another of what to do with you!

MATT: Yeah well I'm goin to keep my mouth shut an wait for Nero because HE will kill me.

TEE: *(Leans down to Matt.)* Not if we get you outta here first.

JAY: Bingo.

TEE: You don't think I can do that?! Two fucken seconds you're over my shoulder an in the car headed to wherever I want you to be headed!

MATT: *(Beat.)* What was the question again?

JAY: He wants to get a sense of what your son might be feelin right now. Am I right, Tee?

(Tee nods.)

MATT: Oh uh, feeling? Well he's probly um...

TEE: You don't know?

MATT: Hey! You didn't know with your boys so, yunno, let up for a minute!

JAY: Just the one kid, right?

(Tee and Jay are practically on top of Matt.)

MATT: Uh actually I got two others in a yunno first marriage. In Arizona. Girls. Both girls.

TEE: Keep talkin, turtle...

MATT: An...I I met my present wife when she was engaged to my then best friend...

JAY: Ooooh-dee-fah, look what we uncovered. Dirt behind dirt.

TEE: "Masks that are skin deep" he said before.

MATT: I…well you can imagine the shit that went down when we fell for each other an then soon after she got pregnant an…I'm not sure if the boy is mine or my ex-best-friend's so I…

JAY: Stayed in the middle about it. Quiet.

MATT: Yeah. Bingo.

TEE: Whadda you, mental? How could you not know?!

MATT: I only see Tip.

JAY: Your ex-best-friend's name is Tip?

MATT: In my minds eye I always see Tip's smile on my son's face an I…

TEE: What's his name?

MATT: Tip.

TEE: No no, I'm talkin about your son.

MATT: Tip. His name is Tip.

JAY: You named your kid afta your ex-best-friend?!

MATT: You're talkin to Al Capone!

TEE: Still, how could you name your kid afta…?!

MATT: AN YOU think your triplets are in jail because you didn't do a ceramics class with 'em so both of you just take a backseat to this fucken conversation CAUSE THIS ONE'S MINE YOU TWO FUCKEN DOPES! YEAH, we named him Tip as a positive start to our marriage, then after the routine set in, I let in my head all this shit an I I couldn't even say his name anymore so I made up my own name for him. When he got a little older, I called him—

(Jay and Tee cover their ears.)

MATT: Wallboy.

(Jay and Tee uncover their ears.)

MATT: He called me…Little Guy…

TEE: Oh God, I'm gonna dump 'im over, that's it— *(Goes to Matt.)* I can't take this fucken clown no more so c'mon Little Guy…

JAY: No No wait wait wait, he's gotta go back. I'm believin it more an more, Tee. He has to go back, he can't die, he has to stand up to all this shit, he really does, I mean listen to this cocksucka, those people he's leavin behind are hurtin, okay, an we caught us a coward runnin an what betta pleasure for us with this prick then to make him face the movie he just escaped from!

TEE: Fuck that. The Little Guy likes young girls and he knew by cuttin into this teenage couple just bein kids was goin to be like plantin a huge fucken bomb, am I right?

MATT: Oh fuck. We back on that Chance versus Choice shit?

TEE: Answer me, turtle!

MATT: I...

TEE: Ya see I think the cryin thing for her is a bunch of crap! I mean at that moment what the fuck is she seein in you?!

MATT: My...tears? Is that what you mean? What is she actually seeing? Or or both our souls, unseen, connecting?

(Tee looks at Jay.)

TEE: It's choice.

(Jay goes to Matt.)

JAY: All right, all right, Sack, answer me this—when you first got her alone, what happened?

MATT: Well lets see, I was givin her a ride home an I could sense this strong pull toward her an an my eyes, my fucken eyes kept blurrin with tears an she says "not peelin onions now" an then I just spilled it all out in this big rush of words, yunno, here I am on route ten tellin a seventeen year old that I'm in love with her and OH FUCK! I'M CAUGHT INBE-TWEEN CHANCE AND CHOICE HERE! SHIT! I mean CHANCE got me cryin an an feelin for her but I made the CHOICE to tell her everything I was goin through!

JAY: *(Leans down to Matt.)* You did that but you'd rather die than open up to your family?

MATT: Unbelievable, isn't it?

TEE: You gambled. You lost. Now you pay. You're just a loser.

MATT: Oh yeah? What about you guys? Huh? How is it you choose to roll people of this dock to their end then go home to your wife and kids?

TEE: Same way a Judge does it.

JAY: Urinologists.

MATT: An your families don't know what it is you do?

TEE: They don't know.

JAY: My Rita, the doll...

TEE: She really is.

JAY: An by the way I did see the scarf. It's ugly as hell.

TEE: Fuck you.

JAY: My Rita tells me an Tee every mornin over coffee how we should relax more in our later years.

(Pause. Sound of lapping water. Men stare out.)

JAY: Jesus, I got Rita leavin, can ya fucken believe it?

TEE: Goin out into the world.

JAY: She adores you. Ugly scarf an all.

TEE: I got it special in Gal-a-lee.

JAY: I saw ya. I was touched. You don't give much.

TEE: *(After a beat.)* You're not gonna really do the Capone thing on Nero, are ya?

JAY: I got to. It's that strong. Undastand me Tee, by me havin this experience with Al Capone, it's shown me there is a place to go to when we get rolled off this dock. To you, a fruity notion, to me it's deep faith cause I know I believe there is more to the life we're seein then just with our eyes.

TEE: *(Puzzled.)* Uh, so…

MATT: He believes in life after death.

TEE: And…

MATT: And he's not afraid to tell that to Nero because now he has faith behind it.

TEE: And…

MATT: AND he's going to need your support because Nero will turn to you afta he hears 'bout Angel Al Capone an want your opinion an won't accept you shrugging your shoulders.

TEE: If you're serious Jay an bring this all up to Nero, you're in the drink before fuckhead!

JAY: I stand by what I've been instructed to do.

TEE: You're dead! That's it! No coffee! No music! No cigars! No tastin! No smellin! He-will-kill-you!

JAY: I stand by my dream.

TEE: No more Rita! How can you follow a dream, a fucken dream message then die for it an give up your family an friends?! How can you do it knowin tamarra that Rita's heart will be broken?!

JAY: What if Nero goes for it?

MATT: You're outta your mind if you think…

TEE: Shut up. *(To Jay.)* If you die, then me as her godfather, makes me her father an what if I fuck up? I mean I don't have a good record, what if I can't handle it?

JAY: If it happens—I trust you can handle it.

TEE: Listen listen uh…you really feel this strong about this whole Capone thing an tellin Nero?

JAY: Yeah, Tee, yeah.

TEE: Okay all right uh okay listen…then let me be the messenger. I'll tell 'im I had the dream.

JAY: You had the dream?

TEE: Lets say that. I had the dream. I talked with Al.

JAY: You'd do that for me? For my dream? You'd do that?

TEE: Yeah. I—I don't know how I'd deal with the Latin Kings anyway an I never done anythin worth anythin.

JAY: So you believe what I been tellin you? All the way?

TEE: You believe it, all the way, right? I mean don't fuck with me at such a sensitive time as this.

JAY: "…its theatre seemed to be his own soul, and events burst in from the outside, violently overcoming the profound resistance of his spirit: passed him through and left him, left the whole cultural structure of a lifetime trampled on, ravaged and destroyed."

MATT: You're actually givin up your life for his dream?

TEE: The man don't lie.

MATT: So I might live because of chance an you're going to maybe die because you choose to. Fuck man, I go out for doughnuts an, wow. Fucken Wow is all I can say.

JAY: Tee. This on the level?

TEE: If not, he'd be in the water, wouldn't he?

JAY: This is a beau-di-ful night.

TEE: Frank, Frankie, and Francis been without me anyways an Mary…she should find herself a a man who can uh yunno, be less um miserable an…then Rita…

JAY: Oh she'll cry hard for you. An I bet that scarf will be with her till the day she dies an it'll be the most beau-di-ful thing on the earth.

TEE: That's kinda nice.

JAY: An I'm gonna make somethin in your honor in my backyard maybe around the bar-ba-que somewheres, no no, by the Bocce court! A memorial for you!

TEE: That's nice, that's nice. To be remembered is a nice feelin down deep. Maybe that's the point, right?

JAY: Exactly! *(Jay recites the following slower and with more feeling.)* That's why you're my reflection you crafty sonofabitch, I love ya ya bastard cause you know, you just know you mother-fucka you do it to me all the time honest to shit you kill me you cocksucka…
(Silence. Jay and Tee stare out.)

MATT: So uh Guys? Is the deal still available? You know, for me to re-enter my life? Cause I'm feelin like I want to go back to…life…to my life an talk with my son an stop only thinkin about myself an I want to turn my wife around from the kitchen sink an just hug her an say somethin nice to her like… "it's okay you wear sweatpants around the house." An then

I want to hold that boy in my arms an say, "I am so proud of you an will love you forever, Tip."

(Tee rises. Picks up the knife from the TV table. Goes to Matt. Bends down. And slits open the sack. Rocks fall out. Tee returns to his lawn chair. Matt stands. He's clad in his underwear, tee-shirt, and socks. He's holding a bag of Dunkin doughnuts. He looks at the Men.)

TEE: Take off. Screw.

JAY: You were the successful object of our moving forward a notch.

TEE: So take off. Screw.

(Matt gets closer to Tee.)

MATT: Um, kinda hard to get a bus to Providence without my pants an…

TEE: Your pants, shoes, an billfold are in the car.

MATT: Okay… *(Matt steps closer to Tee.)*

TEE: *(Without looking at Matt.)* And if you're thinkin a huggin me with only your underwear on, you're gonna die with me.

MATT: Okay, okay, I did want to express somethin for what ya did but…okay… *(Matt starts to leave the dock then stops—He removes two doughnuts from the bag and places them on the TV table then exits.)*
(Jay and Tee sit still looking out to the ocean.)

TEE: Think Nero will come?

JAY: We'll just have to wait an see. He's not here now.

TEE: Right. Only the water an moon in front of us.

JAY: That's it.

(Pause.)

TEE: Jay?

JAY: Tee.

TEE: Latin Kings, huh?

JAY: Yeah Tee, Latin Kings.

(Tee places his arm awkwardly around Jay's shoulder. Not a hug. No squeeze. It's just there. A lively Spanish tune comes up (Ala Gipsy Kings.) and hold on the two men looking out as lights fade—the music increases in volume— and Blackout—

END OF PLAY

The Potato Creek
Chair of Death

BY ROBERT KERR

THE AUTHOR

Robert Kerr's plays include *The End of the Road*, which was workshopped at the Eugene O'Neill Theater Center's National Playwrights Conference in 1997, and *Right for a Dog*, which was produced in Ensemble Studio Theatre's Hell's Kitchen Sink Series. Other plays include *This the Word, The Secret Word for Today is Carrot* and *Six Characters in Search of Water*, which have been produced in Minneapolis, Chicago, Portland, Oregon, and Winter Haven, Florida. He also wrote the book for a musical adaptation of Beatrix Potter's *The Tale of Peter Rabbit* for Child's Play Theatre in Minneapolis. Mr. Kerr was a founding member of Bedlam Theatre in Minneapolis, received two Jerome Fellowships from the Playwrights' Center in Minneapolis, and had two plays produced in the Foundation of the Dramatists Guild's Young Playwrights Festival (one of which was published in *Sparks in the Park and Other Prize-Winning Plays*). He graduated from Macalester College in St. Paul and was a playwright-in-residence at The Juilliard School.

ORIGINAL PRODUCTION

The Potato Creek Chair of Death was first produced at the Ensemble Studio Theatre Marathon '97. It was directed by Richard Caliban, stage manager David Winitsky, with the following cast:

MICHAEL	Gabriel Mann
VALERIE	Janet Zarish
CEDRIC	Chris Ceraso
DIERDRE	Alethea Allen
ELLEN/LINDA/VOICE/CRAZY GUY	Kristin Griffith

AUTHOR'S NOTE

When I was a junior in college, I received a commission from the Playwrights' Center to write a one-act play. At about the same time, I read John Guare's *Landscape of the Body*, a play which completely blew me away. While casting around for ideas for my own play, I remembered a rumor I had heard years earlier about a chair of death somewhere in the American West. Inspired to try writing my own *Landscape of the Body*, I asked myself who might seek out the legendary death chair, and the result was *The Potato Creek Chair of Death*.

In addition to Curt Dempster, Jamie Richards, and everyone else at EST, I'd like to thank Jeffrey Hatcher, Waring Jones, Wendy Knox, Carolyn Petrie, Steve Kaplan, Steven Albrezzi, Mark Roberts, Richard Caliban and the cast of the Marathon production for their help in the development of this play.

CHARACTERS
MICHAEL: who has run away from home
VALERIE: an elderly woman
CEDRIC: her son
DIERDRE: who has also run away from home
ELLEN: who owns a gift shop
LINDA: a waitress
a VOICE: which comes from above
a crazy GUY

SETTING
A gift shop, a highway, a diner, another highway, a gas station, another highway again, a motel, a rest stop, a back road, a scenic overlook, a telephone booth, a barn, still another highway. All in Iowa, Minnesota, and South Dakota.

TIME
Sometime before the year 2000.

SCENE ONE

A souvenir shop. Afternoon. Michael, Cedric and Ellen. Separately, Valerie sitting in a car.

MICHAEL: This kid told me about it in like second grade—

CEDRIC: You got any of those dashboard things—

MICHAEL: I don't even know if it's real or not—

CEDRIC: Those little ladies with the titties that light up?

ELLEN: No, we certainly do not.

MICHAEL: It's like this chair—

CEDRIC: How about those tumblers, you know—

MICHAEL: And it's set up in front of this gun—

CEDRIC: You put ice in and the lady's clothes disappear.

ELLEN: What kind of shop do you think this is?

MICHAEL: This chair and this gun, you see—

CEDRIC: A souvenir shop.

MICHAEL: And the gun's hooked up to a machine—

ELLEN: What you are looking for are not souvenirs.

CEDRIC: Sure they are, if they say, "Hi from Cedar Rapids."

ELLEN: *(To Michael.)* I'm sorry. It's something you heard about in second grade.

MICHAEL: Yeah. It's a chair, like out west somewhere, and there's this gun set up in front of it, and the gun's set to go off sometime between now and the year 2000, but nobody knows when exactly. And people pay money to sit in this chair.

ELLEN: Whatever for?

MICHAEL: I dunno. It's like Russian Roulette, maybe.

CEDRIC: You're tempting fate.

MICHAEL: Yeah. Something like that.

ELLEN: Well, I've never heard of such a thing.

CEDRIC: Sounds like the Potato Creek Chair of Death.

MICHAEL: You've heard of it?

CEDRIC: Been reading this travel guide, about the hundred weirdest tourist traps in America. I decided I wanted to see them all since I won the Publishers Clearing House Sweepstakes.

ELLEN: You won that sweepstakes?

CEDRIC: That's right. Quit my job, sold my house, and now I'm traveling around the country with my Mama. Want her to see all these weird things before she dies. Been to about twelve or—

MICHAEL: I'm looking for that thing, the Potato...whatever, Chair—

CEDRIC: In a place called Potato Creek, South Dakota. Or maybe North Dakota. Can't remember—

MICHAEL: Do you sell maps here?

ELLEN: If I can find them. My husband would know, but he left the other day. The bastard ran off with another woman. Girl, really. She's eighteen years old. Maybe nineteen. The ironic thing is that eight years ago he ran off from his first wife to marry me. We met at the University of Nebraska. I was a grad student looking after the rats in the psychology lab—

MICHAEL: Could I have that map?

ELLEN: Let me check the back room.

(Ellen exits. Michael goes to the window and looks out. He sees Valerie. Valerie senses Michael's gaze. She turns and sees him. They regard each other for a moment.)

MICHAEL: Is that your mother out there in the car?

CEDRIC: Why do you want to know?

MICHAEL: No reason.

(Beat.)

CEDRIC: That your car?

MICHAEL: Yeah.

CEDRIC: Piece a junk.

(Ellen returns.)

ELLEN: He was on the grounds crew. I walked by him one morning while he was raking leaves. He smiled and said hi. I started telling him how I felt trapped, like the rats in the lab—

MICHAEL: Could you—

ELLEN: Don't worry. I haven't forgotten. *(Ellen exits.)*

CEDRIC: You from Ohio, then?

MICHAEL: How'd you know?

CEDRIC: Your plates. Boy are you jumpy. What are you doing in Iowa all by yourself? Run away from home?

MICHAEL: Never mind.

CEDRIC: All right. *(Beat.)* Look at that. Iowa state patrol car pulling into the parking lot.

MICHAEL: Haven't you found that map yet?

ELLEN: *(Offstage.)* I'm looking!

CEDRIC: He's having a pretty good look at your car. I hear Iowa state troopers are pretty tough.

MICHAEL: Really?

ELLEN: *(Offstage.)* Found it!

CEDRIC: Wouldn't know, actually. Just making conversation.

(Ellen returns.)

ELLEN: And he said, "Don't you see? You're not like the rats at all. Your cage is only in your head." So we eloped. Why we came to fucking Iowa and opened a gift shop I'll never know—

MICHAEL: Is that the map?

ELLEN: Yes, but I don't know if you really want it.

MICHAEL: Why not?

ELLEN: It's pretty old. It was in a box that's been here since we bought the place.

MICHAEL: I don't care.

ELLEN: The roads have all probably changed.

MICHAEL: Please. Just give me the map.

ELLEN: There's an Amoco just down the street. They'd have a new one.

CEDRIC: Looks like that trooper's going round to the front.

MICHAEL: *(Laying a bill on the counter.)* Here.

ELLEN: Don't you want your change?

CEDRIC: Coming in the front door.

(Michael exits.)

ELLEN: Wait, that's the back room! Employees only! Use the front—What's wrong with you?

SCENE TWO

Cedric is driving his car. Valerie sits next to him.

CEDRIC: It's so dark, Mama. Not another car around for miles. Feels like we're the only two people in the whole world.

(Pause. In his car, Michael is making up a heavy-metal song.)

MICHAEL: WHATEVER I DID, IT WASN'T ENOUGH
WHATEVER I SAID, IT WAS NEVER THE RIGHT STUFF
WHEREVER I WENT, YOU WERE RIDING MY BACK
WELL, IT'S OVER. IT'S OVER AND DONE
CUZ IT'S THE LAST TIME...

(Lights fade a little on Michael and come up a little on Valerie and Cedric.)

VALERIE: I don't care what you say. I thought he was quite handsome.

CEDRIC: Should have seen him close up. Had things growing in his hair.

VALERIE: What was his name?

CEDRIC: I don't know, Mama. Just some punk running from the police. Did you see that shirt he was wearing? Creepy. Black. Had skulls and things on it.

VALERIE: That kind of thing is just for show. He seemed nice enough to me.

CEDRIC: That boy was running from the law. I bet he was some punk who ran off with his parents' car. I never took anything of yours. I was a good kid. Still am.

(Pause.)

VALERIE: How soon do we stop for the night?

CEDRIC: Next Motel 6.

VALERIE: Why don't we stop somewhere nice for once? Get a suite so I could have my own room? We can afford it.

CEDRIC: What do you need your own room for? I don't have anything you haven't already seen.

VALERIE: Just one suite for one night. My own room. That's all I want.

CEDRIC: What's wrong with Motel 6? They've got those funny commercials on the radio. *(Pause.)* You're not mad at me, are you, Mama? Look, let's compromise. We can stay at a Holiday Inn. It's a step up from Motel 6. Okay? Mama?

(Lights up on Michael.)

MICHAEL: IT'S THE LAST TIME

CEDRIC: Oh, Jesus.

MICHAEL: I HAVE TO LISTEN TO YOU

CEDRIC: Someone's coming up behind us about eighty miles an hour.

MICHAEL: IT'S THE LAST TIME

CEDRIC: Damn people riding on your behind.

MICHAEL: I HAVE TO PUT UP WITH YOU

CEDRIC: Ought to slam on the brakes and teach him a lesson.

MICHAEL: IT'S THE LAST TIME

VALERIE: Settle down, Cedric. Look. He's changed lanes.

MICHAEL: I HAVE TO LOOK AT YOUR FACE

CEDRIC: So he wants to race.

VALERIE: Just let him pass.

MICHAEL: IT'S THE LAST TIME

CEDRIC: I'll show him what this car can do.

VALERIE: Cedric, slow down.

MICHAEL: I HAVE TO SMELL YOUR BREATH

CEDRIC: No one passes me, Mama.

VALERIE: There's a curve ahead. Cedric!

MICHAEL: IT'S THE LAST TIME

VALERIE: Slow down or I'll never speak to you again.

MICHAEL: I HAVE TO...NA NA NA NA

CEDRIC: You happy? Could have passed him if...

MICHAEL: IT'S THE LAST TIME

CEDRIC: Ohio plates.

MICHAEL: THE LAST TIME

VALERIE: What did you say?

CEDRIC: Nothing.

MICHAEL: YEAH!

CEDRIC: Goddamn kids.

MICHAEL: Goddamn old people.

SCENE THREE
A diner. Cedric and Linda. Separately, Valerie in the car.

LINDA: ...and that's what I do. I go someplace, wait tables for a couple months, long enough to save up for a junker car. I drive it until it falls apart and wherever I end up is where I live for the next couple months. I guess maybe someday I'll settle down but not just yet. I really get off on coming to a new town where nobody knows me: I could be anyone. It's like I can pour myself into the corners of my being I never knew were there. You spend too much time with someone and they expect you to act a certain way. Like Jeff, the cook here. I'm staying with him now, you know, and this morning we woke up and he said, "Why didn't you kiss me on the cheek? You kiss me on the cheek every morning." So now I know it's about time to move on. Five thirty-five with tax.

CEDRIC: Here you go.

LINDA: Oh. I don't know if we can change a bill that large.

CEDRIC: Keep the change then. Can't say I'm not a generous man. *(As Cedric turns to go, he bangs his elbow on the counter.)* OW! Shit shit shit shit shit.

LINDA: Oh my God. Are you okay?

CEDRIC: I am going to have one hell of a bruise tonight.

LINDA: Do you want ice or anything?

CEDRIC: No, no. I'll just have Mama give me a shot. *(Cedric sits and waits for the pain to pass.)* It's this damn hemophilia. The doctors say I got it from my Mama. I don't believe it. I love my Mama dearly. My wife left me

about the same time Papa died, so I moved in with Mama. Now we're traveling around the country together. We're real close.
(Michael enters.)
MICHAEL: Can you help me? I'm trying to find Highway 14.
LINDA: Highway 14? I'm not sure.
MICHAEL: This is Rochester, right?
LINDA: Yeah.
MICHAEL: Doesn't it go right through here?
LINDA: I haven't heard of it. I haven't lived here long, though. Do you have a map?
MICHAEL: Here.
LINDA: I don't recognize any of these roads. Let me see if Jeff knows. *(Linda exits.)*
CEDRIC: It's you again. From the gift shop.
MICHAEL: Oh. Yeah.
CEDRIC: Sure left in a hurry when that cop showed up. All he wanted was to check your insurance, you being from Ohio and all. You wanted for something?
MICHAEL: Speeding ticket.
CEDRIC: Figures, the way you passed us last night. Going at least eighty. What's your name? *(Pause.)* Come on, sport. We keep running into each other. We're practically traveling companions.
MICHAEL: My name's Bill.
CEDRIC: Well, Bill, my name's Cedric. Cedric Wedge. You're not looking at my mother, are you?
MICHAEL: I'm looking at your car.
CEDRIC: Nice car, isn't it. Me and Mama were in Chicago and the car broke down, so I just bought a new one. Just like that. You can do things like that when you win the sweepstakes.
MICHAEL: What's her name?
CEDRIC: Tag says Linda.
MICHAEL: What?
CEDRIC: The little tag she wears on her shirt. Says Linda.
MICHAEL: I don't mean the waitress. I mean your mother.
CEDRIC: Her name's Mama.
MICHAEL: Her real name.
CEDRIC: Valerie. But what difference does it make? Look at those hubcaps. Those spoke-like things crossing each other, going in and out—
MICHAEL: She's beautiful.

CEDRIC: Bet you wish you had a car like that.

MICHAEL: I was talking about your mother.

CEDRIC: Oh. It's the way she looks through the windshield. She's sixty-seven. Looks twenty years older in the light though. Real farty, too. Whoo-hoo. You have to roll down the windows when you ride with her. You wouldn't like her much. I can barely stand her myself. Just looking for a good nursing home to put her in. Haven't found one that's medieval enough yet. Medieval! I crack myself up sometimes. You're not laughing. Oh, well. Some people can't appreciate a good joke. Well, I better go. Mama's waiting for me.

(Cedric exits. Linda enters, calling off.)

LINDA: Yeah, Jeff? Yeah? Well, maybe he *will* give me a ride. Maybe I don't kiss you 'cause I'm sick of your ass! *(To Michael.)* Sorry about that. How old is this map, anyway? Jeff says there hasn't been a highway 14 here for years. Anyway, here's where you want to go...

SCENE FOUR

Night. Dierdre on the road, hitchhiking. Cedric and Valerie in their car, lit separately. Dierdre sticks her thumb out.

VALERIE: Look at that girl up ahead. Do you think she needs help?

CEDRIC: It's dangerous to pick up people on the road.

VALERIE: Let's just stop and ask her.

CEDRIC: No. Don't know what kind of crazies go out hitchhiking in the middle of the night.

(Lights fade on Dierdre.)

VALERIE: Did you see her? She couldn't have been much older than nineteen or twenty. Let's go back.

CEDRIC: You always have to go worrying about other people. What's wrong? I'm not enough for you?

VALERIE: I always told Clive it was a mistake to have just one. They get spoiled.

CEDRIC: What was that, Mama? Who gets spoiled?

VALERIE: Only children. Should have spanked you when you were young.

CEDRIC: Don't say that, Mama. You know how easy I bruise. I could have died. You lost Daddy and I lost Marian and the kids. We have to make do with what we've got. All we've got is each other. We can't lose that.

SCENE FIVE

Michael in his car. Dierdre just outside.

DIERDRE: I gotta get to California. Where are you going?

MICHAEL: South Dakota. Potato Creek.

DIERDRE: Can you take me that far? I'm not gonna knife you or anything. I'll even chip in for gas.

(Pause.)

MICHAEL: All right. Get in.

(Dierdre gets in. Michael starts to drive.)

DIERDRE: I'm Dierdre. What's your name?

MICHAEL: Bill.

DIERDRE: So tell me about yourself, Bill. *(Pause.)* Come on. If were going to South Dakota we might as well get to know each other. *(Pause.)* Look, everyone says it's dangerous to hitchhike, especially if you're a girl, but you don't ever get anywhere if you don't trust anyone. I think people are good at heart. So I trust you. You can trust me, too. *(Pause.)* So why are you going to South Dakota?

MICHAEL: I dunno.

DIERDRE: You look like you're about sixteen or something. Are you running
·   away from home?

MICHAEL: Yes.

DIERDRE: My God, so am I. Why did you run away? You couldn't stand your parents?

MICHAEL: Yes.

DIERDRE: Me too. This is so weird. Sometimes I could just kill my parents, you know what I mean? *(Beat.)* Oh, I don't mean really kill them, but sometimes they make me so mad. I mean, my Mom used to be cool but she got divorced and married this real jerk named Alex. God he was a prick. He'd always look at me real funny. I mean like sexy funny. And Mom would never listen to me. So I left. There's nothing to do around here anyway. Small town Minnesota is such a nowhere place. I turned eighteen today. Say "Happy Birthday." I mean it.

MICHAEL: Happy birthday.

DIERDRE: Thank you. So I got up this morning, went up to Mom and Alex and I said, "Today I'm an adult. You can't tell me what to do anymore. I'm leaving home." I mean, it wasn't that big a surprise, because I've been saying I was gonna leave home for the past year, but I guess they never really believed me. But I had my bag on my shoulder and now they saw

I was serious and my Mom started to cry. I was like sad at first, when I got to the end of the driveway, but right now I'm just really happy. I feel like eight feet tall. Nothing can stop me now. Oh my God. It just hit me. I'm going to California. I can't believe it.

SCENE SIX
A self-serve gas station. Later that night. Valerie is in the car. Cedric stands near a pump. He reaches for the nozzle. A voice is heard from above.

VOICE: Number six.
(Cedric stops. He looks around. Beat. Once more he reaches for the nozzle.)
VOICE: Number six.
(Cedric stops again. Beat. Again, he reaches for the nozzle.)
VOICE: Number six.
(Cedric looks at the pump, then looks up.)
CEDRIC: What?
VOICE: Pay before you pump, please.
CEDRIC: Goddamn world. No one trusts you anymore.
(Cedric exits. Lights up on Michael and Dierdre in his car at the next pump. Michael gets out of the car and starts for the pump. He sees Valerie and stops. After a moment he approaches Valerie, who hasn't noticed him yet. He moves to rap on the window. Valerie turns and sees him. Cedric enters.)
CEDRIC: We meet again.
MICHAEL: Yeah.
CEDRIC: Funny how we should keep running into each other.
MICHAEL: Yeah.
CEDRIC: Like you were following us or something.
MICHAEL: Maybe we're just going the same way.
CEDRIC: Interstate's the most direct route. Why don't you take that?
MICHAEL: I dunno. Just never got the hang of those on-off ramps.
CEDRIC: Avoid the cops better, too, I suppose. Any special time you have to be in Potato Creek?
MICHAEL: Not really.
CEDRIC: Me and Mama have got a three hour drive ahead of us. We should get going. We're going to see the giant Paul Bunyan statue. It talks. It's in Bemidji. Up north. You're going west, if you're going to South Dakota. Looks like this is where our paths diverge. Real nice knowing you.

(Cedric gets into his car. Valerie and Michael look at each other as Cedric puts the car in gear. Lights fade on Valerie and Cedric; they are gone. Michael moves toward the pump.)

VOICE: Number eight.

(Michael puts his hand on the nozzle.)

VOICE: Number eight.

(Michael tries to pick up the nozzle. It won't budge.)

VOICE: Number eight. Pay before you pump, please.

SCENE SEVEN

Later that night. Valerie and Cedric in their car.

CEDRIC: What is it you got for that boy, anyhow?

VALERIE: I was only going to say hello, Cedric.

CEDRIC: Am I such a failure as a son you got to go out and find another one? Is that it? He'd be a sweet little thing for you, wouldn't he, with centipedes living in his hair and that stench coming from his armpits? Sure, I bring home a dirty magazine once in a while. I get lonely in certain ways. But him, he's scary. There's something up with him. Something more than a Penthouse under the mattress. Or maybe you want to sleep with him. I see the way you make eyes at each other. Is that it? Think of Daddy. Think of Daddy in his grave.

VALERIE: Why are you bringing Clive up? You always hated him.

CEDRIC: That's beside the point. And it would be wrong. You're at least three times as old as he is. Like mixing buds and dead leaves. Anyway, you're so old you can't feel anything down there anymore.

VALERIE: You have no idea what I feel.

CEDRIC: Leave you in a ditch. See where you'd be then.

VALERIE: Why don't you?

(Pause.)

CEDRIC: All right.

VALERIE: What are you doing?

CEDRIC: Leaving you in the ditch. If you love somebody set them free, so to speak. Well?

VALERIE: Cedric...

CEDRIC: Go on. The door's unlocked.

(Valerie gets out of the car.)

CEDRIC: You can get your suitcase and start going.

(Valerie starts to walk away.)

CEDRIC: Mama...Don't forget your coat! It's kind of chilly tonight. I hope you don't have to walk very far in this cold, dark night out in the middle of nowhere. I hope you find somewhere to settle down. You got any friends in Minnesota?

(Valerie stops.)

CEDRIC: I said, you got any friends in Minnesota? Oh well. Maybe you'll make some. Good luck.

(Pause. Valerie returns.)

CEDRIC: It's nice and warm in here, isn't it? *(Pause.)* Heh-heh. That was a good one. You sure put one over on me. For a minute I thought you were really going to leave. You reminded me of Marian for minute. The exact same thing. I stopped the car. I said, "If you love somebody set them free." She got out of the car and walked away. Into the rain. Never came back. *(Pause.)* You didn't think I was serious, did you Mama? I'd never leave you in the ditch. I swear.

SCENE EIGHT

Dierdre and Michael in his car. Pause.

DIERDRE: Do you believe in God?

MICHAEL: What?

DIERDRE: I'm sorry if that's like a really personal question, but I look at people and I wonder if they believe in God. I just don't know myself, so I get curious. It's just me, I guess.

(Pause.)

MICHAEL: I don't know if there is a God, but the universe is like this big machine, and all the rocks and trees and water and stars and animals and everything is part of this big machine. And people are a part of it too, but they're a part of the machine that got screwed up. Our brains get in the way and we think too much and we don't always do what we're supposed to. In fact, we almost never do it. But the universe knows this and tries to tell us what to do. There are signs if you know how to look for them. Like when I saw you on the highway that meant I was supposed to pick you up. I don't know why yet. Maybe you were sent to help me. Or maybe I'm supposed to help you. Or both.

DIERDRE: Both, I bet. My cousin Marcus is going to help me too. You see, he was going to Harvard like five years ago and he was gonna be a doctor and everything. But he hated it and one day he just walked out of class and sold his stereo and used the money to go to California. Now he works for a record company. He knows all these famous people and he makes like fifty thousand a year.

So now I'm going to California and ask Marcus to get me a job. He doesn't know I'm coming yet, but he's gonna help me. I know he is. He's real cool. I'm not that smart and I'm not that pretty so it's not like things are just going to land in front of me. I better do something, even if it's a bit crazy. I mean, sometimes I just wanna do something really crazy just to prove that I can do it, you know what I mean?

MICHAEL: Yeah.

DIERDRE: I've always wanted to, like, go skinny dipping.

MICHAEL: Sometimes when I'm driving at night, like right now, I see the white line going by on the right and the yellow line on the left, and everything's just the darkness and those lines that I'm staying between. And I start wondering what would happen if I turned the wheel to the right and drove over the white line into the darkness—

DIERDRE: This is starting to give me the creeps.

MICHAEL: I mean, I know I *can* do it, I can turn the wheel, and what's stopping me? It's like just rules that stop you—

DIERDRE: Stop it.

MICHAEL: and rules aren't real. People just made them up. But if I follow those rules, I wonder if that makes me more unreal than the rules.

DIERDRE: I wanna get out now.

MICHAEL: I guess maybe I'm scared of hitting a tree so I stay on the road. But still, sometimes I come so close to just turning the wheel.

DIERDRE: Please stop the car.

MICHAEL: Just to see what would happen. Just to see if I'm—

DIERDRE: STOP THE CAR!

(Dierdre reaches her foot over and steps on the brake. She steers the car to the side of the road and gets out of the car.)

MICHAEL: Wait. Wait! I was just saying, just saying what if!

(Dierdre is gone.)

SCENE NINE

The next evening. Michael in a motel room. There is a knock at the door. Pause. Knocking again, more urgent.

CEDRIC: *(Offstage.)* I know you're in there. I see the light on. Open up. I want to talk. *(Pause.)* My Mama's out here too. She wants to talk to you. *(Michael opens the door. Cedric barges in.)*

MICHAEL: Where is she?

CEDRIC: I lied. That's how I figured I could get you to the door, the way you've been sniffing around her. What is it? The smell of rot turns you on? Ben-Gay? You're seventeen years old. Find someone your own age. Shouldn't be hard. You're a TV star now.

MICHAEL: What?

CEDRIC: How does it feel to have your face on hundreds of thousands of TV screens across the country? How does it feel to be famous? I thought I'd have to wait to watch it on the news, but now I get to see it right here when they take you away. You see, I'm staying in a room right around the corner, and just five or ten minutes ago I was kicking back watching America's Most Wanted, one of my favorite shows, and they showed the face of a boy. A seventeen-year-old boy from Ohio named Michael who is wanted by the authorities for the murder of his parents.

MICHAEL: Oh my God.

CEDRIC: I picked up the phone and dialed the number. 1-800-HOT-TIPS. It was busy. Oh well. I think I'll go get some ice for my Coca-Cola and come back and try calling again. I was standing at the ice machine and I turned around and looked down from the balcony, and what do you think I saw? *(Pause.)* Well? Tell me what you think I saw.

MICHAEL: I don't know.

CEDRIC: I love this. I feel like a character on Dynasty. What I saw was this: a car with Ohio plates. It was too good to be true. I just had to drop in and say hello. See how you were. Now, if you'll excuse me, I have a phone call to make. *(Cedric exits.)*

SCENE TEN

Cedric and Valerie's hotel room, immediately afterward. Valerie is present. Cedric enters.

CEDRIC: Mama, you won't believe this. I just saw that Bill character. The Michael kid from the T.V. show.

VALERIE: Where is he?

CEDRIC: He'll be long gone if I don't call the cops. I was coming back from the ice machine and...Mama, where's the phone? *(Pause.)* Mama.

(Pause.) I have to call the police on him. You saw the show. He's cold-blooded. Don't feel safe with him so close by. Could be you or me next. *(Pause.)* Mama, this isn't funny anymore. *(Pause.)* Is this to get back at me for the ditch thing? I said I'm sorry, Mama. It was a joke. I apologize. *(Pause.)* Mama, you've hardly said two words since then. You all right? I'm getting concerned. *(Pause.)* WHERE'S THE GODDAMN PHONE?

VALERIE: I smashed it into little pieces and flushed it down the toilet.

CEDRIC: When?

VALERIE: While you were out.

CEDRIC: You didn't. You wouldn't. I know you. *(Pause.)* I know. Let's play warmer-colder with the phone. I'll walk around the room and you say "warmer" when I'm getting close and so on. Just like we played when I was little. All right?

(Cedric starts to move around the room. Valerie says "warmer" as Cedric approaches her and "colder" as he moves away from her.)

VALERIE: Warmer...warmer...colder...colder...freezing cold...warmer... warmer...warmer...colder...colder...warmer...warmer...warmer...hot ...hotter...burning up.

(Valerie raises her arm to strike Cedric. Blackout.)

SCENE ELEVEN

A rest stop with a kiosk. Night. A crazy Guy and Michael.

GUY: YEEEEEOWWWWWW!...cars and cars and YEEEEEOWWW! There goes another one and cars and trucks and riding by looking out at the road going by

MICHAEL: Hello.

GUY: and faces...faces go by so fast so...YEEEEOWWWWW! That was close. Too close. Too close for comfort.

MICHAEL: Excuse me—

GUY: gonna kill us all someday run over and bam on the road

MICHAEL: I'm trying—

GUY: all over and flat flat as a pancake flat like you're in a movie which is what it's like

MICHAEL: I'm trying to get to South Dakota.

GUY: that's what it looks like in a car speeding speeding by the world at ninety miles an hour and that's life

MICHAEL: I'm lost. My map's all wrong.

GUY: life it's life watching people through a car window like a movie YEEE-OWWWWW! Don't you see them? That one almost hit you YEEE-OWWWW!

MICHAEL: Is this a map, in this thing?

GUY: Look out! YEEEOWWWWW!

MICHAEL: I'm just going to, you know...

GUY: YEEOWWW! YEEEOWWW! YEEOWWW!

MICHAEL: ...look at this map thing.

(Michael goes to the kiosk. The crazy guy follows him.)

GUY: like a movie they go by so fast and for just a moment you look into their lives...a mother beats a little boy...two guys hug each other...that's all you see, that one moment, and to us that's all they are, she's a child abuser they're queers and they're gone and of course they're more than that—

MICHAEL: Well, have a good—

GUY: She's president of the PTA and one of them plays jazz every Thursday

MICHAEL: A good night.

GUY: and the other goes to trade school in the day, but you'd never know

MICHAEL: I've gotta go.

GUY: because we see these like they're outtakes from longer movies

MICHAEL: Sorry.

GUY: but we never get to see the whole thing

(Michael exits.)

GUY: YEEEEOWWWW! watch where you're going stay on the road oh my God look out it's a semi a giant semi coming closer closer CLOSER! He's slamming on his BRAKES look OUT closer closer squealing SCREEE! slamming on his brakes SCREEE! SCREEE! *SCREEEEEE!!!!!!*

SCENE TWELVE

Lights change suddenly to Michael getting out of his car and Valerie standing in front of it.

MICHAEL: Are you all right?

VALERIE: My God.

MICHAEL: I'm sorry. You just came out of nowhere.

VALERIE: Who are you?

MICHAEL: It's so dark I didn't—

VALERIE: I can't see. Your headlights—

MICHAEL: Valerie?

VALERIE: What?

MICHAEL: Is that you?

VALERIE: How do you know my name?

MICHAEL: It's me. Michael. From the gift shop. The gas station. Is that blood?

VALERIE: Oh my God! Where?

MICHAEL: On your—

VALERIE: It's...it's...It's Cedric's...They'll find the car in the morning. I have to be far away. You have to help me.

MICHAEL: How?

VALERIE: You have to understand. He always...He had this way of...Whenever he was around there was hardly room for me to even breathe—

MICHAEL: What happened? Where is he?

VALERIE: He wanted to use the phone, but I wouldn't let him. I hit him hard on the nose. He has hemophilia. I knew that, but in that split second I forgot. I hit him all over. I just didn't stop. He had bruises everywhere. He was so surprised and so delicate he didn't stop me. He just collapsed and started to cry. I stopped and said I'd take him to the hospital. I did-n't know where the hospital was, of course, but I was so scared and so sad and so confused I thought we could just keep driving until we found it. He was sitting next to me with blood coming out of his nose and his skin turning funny colors. After a while I noticed he had stopped crying. He was just sitting up in the seat. Not moving. So I just kept driving until the car ran out of gas. *(Pause.)* I did love him, I think. I don't know. As bad as...as awful as this sounds...When I was hitting Cedric, and hit-ting him and hitting him...Something came from somewhere, while I was hitting him. A feeling, not since I was...Something I thought was lost forever. Something alive. I can't let it waste away. I can't get caught. I need you to give me a ride. Wherever you are going.

MICHAEL: I'm not going past South Dakota.

VALERIE: As long as we'll be safe.

MICHAEL: All right.

SCENE THIRTEEN
Later that night. Michael and Valerie in his car.

VALERIE: Were you really following us?

MICHAEL: Not at first. But it was like a sign, when I kept running into you.

(Pause.)

VALERIE: When I was your age, young men didn't pierce their ears.

MICHAEL: Yeah?

(Pause.)

VALERIE: I'm not saying it looks bad.

(Pause.)

MICHAEL: Well, you dress good for an old lady...I'm sorry. I didn't mean old.

VALERIE: That's all right. I am old.

MICHAEL: What I mean is you don't wear lots of polyester and stuff. And you're pretty.

VALERIE: Thank you.

SCENE FOURTEEN

A scenic overlook. Just before dawn. Michael is sitting in the car, reading a map. Valerie is outside.

VALERIE: Michael, you can see South Dakota across the river from here. Look at it. You can just barely make out the far bank.

(Michael comes out of the car.)

VALERIE: Doesn't it feel good to stretch your legs after driving all night?

MICHAEL: Yeah.

(Pause.)

VALERIE: What are we going to do once we're in South Dakota?

MICHAEL: I don't know. Finding you wasn't part of the plan.

VALERIE: I'm sorry if I'm—

MICHAEL: No. I don't mean that. You must have been a part of the plan I didn't know about.

VALERIE: What plan?

MICHAEL: The plan for my life. What I'm meant to do. I feel like I'm reading the signs all wrong. It wasn't me that killed my parents, right? It was the universe. I was just a tool. They were meant to die. I just did what should do.

I mean, when I got up at two in the morning and I was really thirsty so I went downstairs and I was looking for the orange juice pitcher, it was a sign when I opened the cupboard where Mom kept the rat poison. I wasn't thinking about it. I just opened it by mistake. Except it wasn't a mistake because the universe does things like that—gets in your brain and makes you do things. I didn't know right away what I should do with the poison. But I knew it was either them or me.

I had to make sure I did the right thing, so I made the orange juice and poured it into two cups that looked exactly the same and put the poison in one of them. I closed my eyes and switched them around a bunch of times and spun myself around so I was really dizzy. I kept my eyes closed and took one of the cups and drank it. I felt kind of sick, but I didn't know if I drank the one with the poison so I poured the other cup back into the pitcher and went to bed.

I couldn't fall asleep right away, but I didn't feel as sick after a while. Then I thought maybe I should tell my parents about the poison. But it was like too much trouble to get them up at three in the morning. I turned off the alarm because if I woke up on my own in time I was meant to save their lives.

I fell asleep and I dreamed about the Chair of Death which I heard about in second grade. I woke up and I wasn't...So they were...I got the car. I started driving. I knew I had to find the Chair of Death because I had that dream about it. And now I feel like I'm Charles Manson or something, because I guess compared to other parents mine weren't all that bad. They never hit me. They never grabbed for my crotch. They never did anything. I never did anything. We all just sat around doing nothing. It was like we were all already dead, so what difference does it make if I really did kill them, right?

(Pause. Valerie takes Michael in her arms.)
VALERIE: Look, we're almost in South Dakota now. We're almost there.

SCENE FIFTEEN
Dierdre at a pay phone.

DIERDRE: Hi, my name is Dierdre Walken. I was watching your show in a Radio Shack in Mankato, and...Mankato, Minnesota. And that guy, Michael what's-his-name? The one who killed his parents? Well, I was hitchhiking a few days ago and this creepy guy picked me up about ten miles from Red Wing, and it was him. He told me his name was Bill, but I recognized him from the picture...He said he was going to South Dakota. Tomato River, or something...No, that's not it...Potato Creek. That's it. Well, I don't really have a phone here...Wait... *(Reading the number on the pay phone.)* Area code 507, 482-6983. Oh, and the reward money. How soon do I get it? Well, if you do, could you wire it to the Western Union in Mankato? And can I keep calling back to see how it's going, in case you can't reach me? I hope you find him soon. I really need the money. I'm trying to get to California. It's starting to get real cold here in Minnesota and I don't even have a coat.

SCENE SIXTEEN

An abandoned barn. A large machine is barely discernible in the darkness. There is the sound of someone attempting to open a door.

VALERIE: *(Offstage.)* Maybe it's locked.

MICHAEL: *(Offstage.)* Just a minute. I think I've got it.

(The door bangs open. Silence. Michael and Valerie enter.)

VALERIE: I don't think this is a good idea.

MICHAEL: I told you, I just want to look at it. That's all.

VALERIE: That book Cedric had said this was shut down years ago. Don't you think they would have taken it apart?

(From the machine there is a click, and then the sound of gears grinding perilously into a new position. Silence.)

VALERIE: What was that?

MICHAEL: I don't know. I think I found the light.

(A single bulb in the rafters snaps on, dimly illuminating the machine. It is the Chair of Death. From the bowels of the machine emerge sporadic ticks and clicks and the sound of springs unwinding. Michael examines the machine.)

VALERIE: All right, you've seen it. Let's go.

MICHAEL: Not yet. *(Indicating a plaque on the wall.)* What does that say?

(Valerie goes to read the plaque. Her back is turned toward Michael.)

VALERIE: "The Chair of Death was built in 1901 by Michael McAfee—"

MICHAEL: We have the same first name.

VALERIE: "apparently as a deranged response to the death of his mother the year before. After completing the device, Mr. McAfee would allow thrill-seekers, for a fee of fifty cents, to sit in the chair for one minute. The Chair of Death consists of a chair, a gun—" Well, we can see that…"It is set to pull the trigger at some undisclosed point in time before the year 2000…"

(Michael sits in the chair.)

VALERIE: Listen to this. "The despondent Mr. McAfee was often found in the small hours of the morning sitting in the device he had constructed, leading some to believe he had actually built it as an instrument of his own death. He died unexpectedly in an automobile accident in 1923, at the age of forty-two. The gun never fired in his lifetime." The poor, poor man. *(Valerie turns toward Michael.)*

VALERIE: Michael, what are you doing? Get out of that chair. Michael!

MICHAEL: Leave me alone.

VALERIE: You said you only wanted to see this thing. You told me—

MICHAEL: Be quiet!

VALERIE: You don't know when that gun is going to go off!

MICHAEL: Yes I do.

VALERIE: You can't possibly—

MICHAEL: I just know.

VALERIE: When?

MICHAEL: Any second now. You sit in the chair for one minute. That's how it works.

VALERIE: How do you know it hasn't gone off already? How do you even know it's still loaded?

MICHAEL: All the signs—

VALERIE: What signs?

MICHAEL: The dreams, running into Cedric at just the right time…I was meant to come here. It's what I deserve. I'm staying here. Just go.

VALERIE: You can't leave me alone, Michael. I think I hear sirens.

(Faint sirens.)

VALERIE: Oh dear God. You have to come. You don't want to get caught.

MICHAEL: The gun will go off first.

VALERIE: What is the chance—

MICHAEL: It has to.

VALERIE: that in one hundred years—

MICHAEL: It has to.

VALERIE: it will go off tonight? Come on.

(Valerie tries to pull Michael from the chair. He throws her to the ground. Michael waits for the gun to go off. Valerie watches. Pause.)

MICHAEL: I'll flip a coin. That'll tell me what to do. Heads I stay, tails I go. *(Michael flips a coin. He looks at it.)* Heads.

VALERIE: Michael, let's go.

MICHAEL: You go. I'm staying. I mean it.

(Valerie starts to leave, but hesitates at the doorway. Unseen by Michael, she lingers at the threshold, looking out. Michael closes his eyes and waits for the

gun to fire. Long pause. The sirens grow louder. Michael opens his eyes. He flips the coin several times in succession.)

MICHAEL: Heads. Heads. Heads.

(He prepares to flip the coin again. He hesitates. Valerie turns to look at Michael. He senses her gaze on him. He turns to look at her. They regard each other. Pause.)

SCENE SEVENTEEN
Valerie and Michael in the car. Michael is driving.

VALERIE: ...and we'll find a small town no one's ever heard of and settle down. In Saskatchewan. We'll get jobs in a restaurant. Or a gas station.

MICHAEL: Maybe they're still building a pipeline somewhere way up north.

VALERIE: You will be my grandson. Cedric had two girls, but he hasn't bothered to see them in years. I miss them. So you will be my grandson. At least, that is the face we'll put on for the people in the small town in Saskatchewan. At night, when we're home by ourselves, we'll make dinner for each other and sit together on the couch and watch the brown autumn leaves drift past the window.

(Pause.)

MICHAEL: I'll like that.

(Pause. Sirens heard, distantly. Michael and Valerie join hands. Michael accelerates. They are going about eighty miles an hour. They keep on driving. Lights fade.)

END OF PLAY

Patronage

BY ROMULUS LINNEY

THE AUTHOR
Romulus Linney is the author of three novels, sixteen long and twenty short plays, staged throughout the United States and abroad. They include *The Sorrows of Frederick, Holy Ghosts, Childe Byron, Heathen Valley* and *"2."* He has won two Obie Awards, two National Critics Awards, three DramaLogue Awards, Fellowships from the NEA, Rockefeller and Guggenheim Foundations, and the Award in Literature from the American Academy and Institute of Arts and Letters, among others. He teaches playwrights in the Actors Studio MFA Program at the New School.

ORIGINAL PRODUCTION
Patronage was originally produced at The Ensember Studio Theatre, May 1997. It was directed by Tom Bullard, Assistant Director Chris Ruston, Stage Manager Hilary Adams, with the following cast:

Husband . . . . Dan Ziskie
Wife . . . . Dana Reeve
Musician . . . . Chris Noth
Visitor . . . . Marc Romero

CHARACTERS
HUSBAND
WIFE
MUSICIAN
VISITOR

PLACE
A music room in a wealthy home in an American city.

TIME
The present

Sofa, chairs, rug, cocktail table. Bottle of Lillet, ice bucket, glasses. Over the sofa hangs an elegant but empty frame for a large painting. Downstage is another beautiful structure, a simple standing piece of wood, with a shelf facing upstage, and a piano bench behind it. This represents a Bosendorfer piano. Lights discover Husband and Wife, waiting. Husband is in a tuxedo. Wife is in an elegant gown and shoulder wrap.

HUSBAND: *When* did he say??

WIFE: At five.

HUSBAND: It's five fifteen

WIFE: He's always a little late starting.

HUSBAND: When you go work with him, all right. We have to go by six.

WIFE: *(Reading.)* We'll make it.

HUSBAND: You sure?

WIFE: Yes! Relax.

HUSBAND: All right.

> *(Doorbell. Wife gets up, exits. Husband waits, thinking. Enter Wife, with Musician, who is dressed informally but neatly.)*

WIFE: Here he is!

MUSICIAN: Sorry I'm late.

HUSBAND: That's quite all right.

WIFE: My husband.

MUSICIAN: Sir!

> *(They shake hands.)*

HUSBAND: I'm very glad to meet you. Some Lillet?

MUSICIAN: Yes, thanks. What a wonderful room!

HUSBAND: We like it. *(He pours wine for all three.)*

MUSICIAN: That painting.

HUSBAND: My wife knows the artist.

MUSICIAN: Really?

WIFE: I found her in SoHo gallery before she was famous. Before SoHo was, either. We helped her along.

HUSBAND: The difference in my wife's playing is extraordinary. How did you do it?

MUSICIAN: Her talent!

HUSBAND: Your lessons!

MUSICIAN: *(Looking at piano.)* And your Bosendorfer. What a gorgeous instrument.

HUSBAND: My mother's.

WIFE: Music, the language of joy.

HUSBAND: So what are you two going to play for me? Something of yours, I hope.

MUSICIAN: God, no.

HUSBAND: Why not?

MUSICIAN: I've never written anything for four hands. Hard to do.

HUSBAND: You're cautious.

MUSICIAN: No, cowardly.

WIFE: Let's try the Schubert.

MUSICIAN: This? *(He shows the Wife some sheet music.)*

WIFE: Oh, yes!

(The Musician and the Wife sit on the piano bench, facing us. They place their hands on the shelf, move their arms, bodies, etc, as if playing, with serious effort, both very capable. Music: the famous Schubert first Marche Militaire, for four hands. The Husband listens, nodding, smiling. They play. The Husband watches them. The Wife makes a mistake, stops. Music stops.)

WIFE: I always do that.

MUSICIAN: Never mind. Here?

WIFE: Yes!

(They continue, the Husband watching. The Musician and the Wife play with a sudden excited flourish. They are both aroused and happy.)

MUSICIAN: Good!

WIFE: There! Oh, that's such fun!

MUSICIAN: Yes, isn't it?

(They play.)

WIFE: Isn't this wonderful?

HUSBAND: Amazing!

WIFE: Wheeee!

MUSICIAN: Good!

HUSBAND: Good!

WIFE: *(Laughing.)* What fun!

MUSICIAN: Good!

WIFE: It's like flying!

MUSICIAN: Then fly!

WIFE: Whee!

MUSICIAN: Good!

WIFE: Oh, good!

(The Wife and the Musician finish. They are exhilarated. Music ends. The Husband applauds, quietly.)

WIFE: Oh, my!

MUSICIAN: You did very well!

WIFE: Really?

HUSBAND: *(Dry.)* Bravo. *(To the Musician.)* You have done her worlds of good.

MUSICIAN: I hope so!

HUSBAND: Have another drink. *(He pours Lillet again.)* To music, the language of joy!

WIFE: To music!

MUSICIAN: To music!

(They drink, smiling at each other.)

HUSBAND: You're doing, evidently, damn fine work.

MUSICIAN: Thank you.

HUSBAND: Teach, concerts. Fellowships, grants.

MUSICIAN: Yes.

HUSBAND: In the papers, uh, what was it?

MUSICIAN: My opera.

HUSBAND: Religious, right?

MUSICIAN: Yes.

HUSBAND: Ambitious.

MUSICIAN: Well, yes.

WIFE: Who's writing the libretto?

MUSICIAN: I am.

HUSBAND: Man of many parts.

MUSICIAN: Yes.

HUSBAND: Have you recorded anything?

MUSICIAN: Yes.

HUSBAND: On tapes?

MUSICIAN: Yes.

HUSBAND: CD's?

MUSICIAN: Both.

HUSBAND: Tower Records?

MUSICIAN: Yes.

HUSBAND: I mean, if I go look behind those little white cards, with Tchaikovsky and Brahms and Beethoven and Bach on them, I'll find you?

MUSICIAN: Yes.

HUSBAND: How many times?

MUSICIAN: Once.

HUSBAND: What?

MUSICIAN: A piano quintet and a horn concerto and the overture to my opera.

HUSBAND: Are they any good?

MUSICIAN: A few think so.

HUSBAND: A few who?

MUSICIAN: Other musicians, I suppose. I'm not that well known.

HUSBAND: A hard profession.

MUSICIAN: Yes.

HUSBAND: So when's the concert?

WIFE: We haven't decided.

MUSICIAN: A few months, maybe.

HUSBAND: You could have it here. It's for the hospital, a good cause.

WIFE: Really, darling? I thought we should rent a place.

HUSBAND: Great evening. All our friends, and then some. Use the house. We could open the ballroom.

WIFE: Really? Darling, wonderful!

HUSBAND: Why not? You've settled on a fee?

MUSICIAN: More than satisfactory.

HUSBAND: A program?

MUSICIAN: She'll do Scarlatti first.

HUSBAND: Easier than Bach.

MUSICIAN: Then I'll do some Bach.

HUSBAND: Of course.

MUSICIAN: She does two Chopin nocturnes, I do a Schubert waltz, she does two Debussy Preludes, then a four hands sonata by Ruher, a young composer in Boston. A dash of Aaron Copeland, Virgil Thomson, and Ned Rorem. Then one rousing encore with the Marche Militaire.

HUSBAND: About a hour?

MUSICIAN: No longer.

HUSBAND: You've thought it through. Very professional.

MUSICIAN: Well, I'll say goodnight, then.

WIFE: Goodnight.

HUSBAND: Wait a minute.

MUSICIAN: Yes, sir?

WIFE: Darling, we'll be late.

HUSBAND: It's my money, they can wait. I just want to ask him something.

MUSICIAN: Ask away.

HUSBAND: What do you think about Marian Anderson?

MUSICIAN: What do you mean, what do I think about Marian Anderson?

HUSBAND: Could she really sing?

MUSICIAN: Yes.

HUSBAND: Paul Robeson?

MUSICIAN: What?

HUSBAND: Playing Othello in London, screwing Lord Mountbatten's wife, who loved alternate sex, but what else? What about Glenn Gould?

MUSICIAN: Glenn Gould?

HUSBAND: He created the art, or practice, of concerts by recordings. I mean, was that honest or not?

MUSICIAN: Marian Anderson had a grand voice. She was the soul of nobility. Cheated, in many ways, of her career, but she suffered that with great self-respect. Paul Robeson made a fuss, and should have. His life and struggle accomplished wonderful things. Lord Mountbatten's wife, whatever else she did, died I believe running the British Red Cross, and was deeply respected. I can hear, in Glenn Gould, separate and at the same time, everything Bach or Berg wanted me to hear. No one, with the exception of an orchestra conductor named Jonel Perlea, did that, that well, and Perlea didn't record much. What's all this about?

HUSBAND: I never heard of Jonel Perlea, we can leave Mountbatten's wife to heaven, but Glenn Gould was overrated. I mean, really, I don't mind a few mistakes, prefer them actually, in a living concert. Gould cut all that up into re-recording everything, choosing from fifty, the perfect trill. Frankenstein music. He was a coward, afraid of his public.

MUSICIAN: He was the greatest pianist of the twentieth century.

HUSBAND: You think so?

MUSICIAN: Yes! The beauty—and precision—and devotion of Glenn Gould's masterful—

HUSBAND: All right, he could play. But that's all. The genius of the keyboard couldn't compose! He could play but HE COULDN'T CREATE!

MUSICIAN: So what?

HUSBAND: You create. I mean, you're writing an opera.

MUSICIAN: So fucking *what?*

HUSBAND: I've made you angry. Because you're Jewish?

WIFE: Oh, God. Darling.

MUSICIAN: *What?*

HUSBAND: Glenn Gould's music. You're a Jew and you know.

MUSICIAN: No, I'm not.

HUSBAND: Not what?

MUSICIAN: I'm not a Jew. Neither was Glenn Gould.

HUSBAND: Gould? He wasn't? Gould?

MUSICIAN: He was a Scottish Presbyterian.

WIFE: God. Darling.

HUSBAND: Really?

MUSICIAN: Did you think I was a Jew?

HUSBAND: You're musical. I assumed it. My wife isn't a Jew, or musical for that matter.

WIFE: Well!

HUSBAND: Not professionally, darling, I mean.

MUSICIAN: Sir, Van Cliburn is musical. So is Leontyne Price. I beg your pardon, folks, but do you dislike people because of race, religion or things like that?

WIFE: Nothing like that!

HUSBAND: Really.

WIFE: We love everybody.

HUSBAND: Almost everybody.

WIFE: Tremendously.

HUSBAND: Like women.

MUSICIAN: Women?

HUSBAND: Equally subjects of oppression. The Nazis treated Jews like women. That's the way they thought of them. That's the real reason why they shot them and gassed them and murdered them. That's why Israelis are so macho today and who can blame them?

MUSICIAN: You are off the mother fucking wall.

HUSBAND: I make perfect sense.

MUSICIAN: Your husband is calling Jewish women a reason for World War II?

WIFE: Well, of course not.

MUSICIAN: Sounds like it.

WIFE: No.

HUSBAND: Call me a sexist racist, do you?

WIFE: Oh, no, darling.

HUSBAND: From head to toe.

MUSICIAN: Well, I wouldn't say that.

HUSBAND: Yes, you would.

MUSICIAN: Well, maybe I would.

WIFE: My husband didn't mean to insult you.

HUSBAND: I beg your pardon, really.

WIFE: I married him against the wishes of my father, who was an Episcopal priest.

HUSBAND: He said I'd never amount to anything. I was too stupid. Do you think I'm stupid?

MUSICIAN: No.

HUSBAND: What do you think I am?

MUSICIAN: Resourceful, powerful, erudite, amazing, shall I say more?

HUSBAND: You know what I mean!

MUSICIAN: You are a man who helps the arts, with a fortune you earned.

HUSBAND: Why?

MUSICIAN: Why what?

HUSBAND: Why do I help the arts with the fortune I earned?

MUSICIAN: Before I met you, I would have hoped because you love what it does for human beings.

HUSBAND: I love my country, too, and what it does for human beings.

MUSICIAN: So do I. What's the contradiction?

HUSBAND: What do you think about my wife?

MUSICIAN: I beg your pardon?

HUSBAND: What is she? Come on.

MUSICIAN: She is an accomplished amateur pianist.

HUSBAND: Is that all?

WIFE: We'll miss the party. You have to make a speech.

HUSBAND: I don't care. We need to have this out.

MUSICIAN: Have what out?

HUSBAND: You and my wife.

(Pause.)

WIFE: Oh, Harold, really.

HUSBAND: Not that I mind. I owe her something. I work late. On the phone through dinner. She's a magnificent hostess to revolting people. To whom we must always seem not *quite* as intelligent as *they* are. Do you think men who make as much money as I do are really very intelligent? Where it counts? As intelligent as artists, I mean?

MUSICIAN: It's time for me to go.

HUSBAND: Chicken.

WIFE: Tell him the truth.

MUSICIAN: Your wife and I are *friends!*

HUSBAND: Define friends.

MUSICIAN: A friend in need is a friend indeed. Your wife is in need!

WIFE: Which he knows!

HUSBAND: Which I know!

MUSICIAN: I'm out of here this minute.

HUSBAND: What do you really think about Aaron Copeland.

MUSICIAN: What?

HUSBAND: Just answer the question.

MUSICIAN: To hell with you!

WIFE: He doesn't have to!

MUSICIAN: Well, I will. *What* was it?

HUSBAND: What do you really think about Aaron Copeland?

MUSICIAN: Clever, and obvious.

HUSBAND: Virgil Thomson?

MUSICIAN: Fine for Gertrude Stein.

HUSBAND: Ned Rorem?

MUSICIAN: Writes good diaries!

HUSBAND: Wolpe, Glass, your friend Ruher in Boston?

MUSICIAN: Am I a better composer? Yes! Than all five! Yes!

HUSBAND: Your opera.

MUSICIAN: What about it?

HUSBAND: Funded?

MUSICIAN: Yes.

HUSBAND: By our government?

MUSICIAN: Yes.

HUSBAND: By American citizens. Their tax. Their sweat, and hard work. Whether they like opera or not. Whether they even know what opera is or not. They pay you, who can't make a living. You, who call three great American composers, who did make a living, less than you!

MUSICIAN: Oh, brother.

HUSBAND: Yes or no?

MUSICIAN: Great countries support the arts.

HUSBAND: I believe that.

MUSICIAN: Well?

HUSBAND: But what is Art?

MUSICIAN: Oh, shit.

HUSBAND: That's my question. It is addressed to you.

MUSICIAN: I bet.

HUSBAND: Do you have an answer?

MUSICIAN: Yes, but you won't like it.

HUSBAND: Try me.

MUSICIAN: Art is life naked.

HUSBAND: What a bromide. Not everything naked is beautiful.

MUSICIAN: Oh, yes, it is.

HUSBAND: You think so?

MUSICIAN: Right.

HUSBAND: *(To his Wife.)* Right?

WIFE: I'm sure I don't know. I haven't been naked. He's been most helpful and kind, giving me piano lessons, which I loved, and you are tearing that all up!

HUSBAND: And what else?

WIFE: Harold!

HUSBAND: Life naked? That's what's beautiful?

WIFE: I told you, Harold!!

HUSBAND: Just taking piano lessons.

WIFE: Yes! And I want to talk about something else! His opera!

HUSBAND: OK!

WIFE: What's it about?

HUSBAND: You don't know?

WIFE: Well, no.

HUSBAND: You want to tell her or shall I?

MUSICIAN: I'll let you do it.

HUSBAND: What the paper said was, it's about Jesus Christ.

WIFE: Really?

MUSICIAN: Really.

HUSBAND: Anybody ever write an opera about Jesus Christ before?

MUSICIAN: Nope.

HUSBAND: You're the first?

MUSICIAN: Oratorios. Passion Plays. No opera.

WIFE: Wonderful!

MUSICIAN: I think so.

WIFE: Is there a title?

MUSICIAN: THE LINEN CLOTH.

WIFE: The what?

HUSBAND: Linen what?

MUSICIAN: Cloth. Linen cloth.

HUSBAND AND WIFE: Oh.

> *(Pause.)*

WIFE: What linen cloth?

MUSICIAN: It's complicated!

HUSBAND: So tell us!

WIFE: Please.

MUSICIAN: A fragment of a letter was found in the back binding of a medieval book. Part of a letter from Clement, a Father of the early Church, saying for God's sake don't let Carpocrates—a rival Jesus—don't let Carpocrates get hold of X.

WIFE: X?

MUSICIAN: The original gospel of which Mark, Matthew and Luke are censored copies.

WIFE: Are what?

MUSICIAN: Censored copies. There was another, original gospel, we don't have. We call it X.

HUSBAND: All right. So, what would Carpocrates have done with X?

MUSICIAN: Use its secrets.

WIFE: What secrets?

MUSICIAN: Sex secrets.

HUSBAND: Sure.

WIFE: Get him out of here.

HUSBAND: Not now! Come on!

MUSICIAN: Mark. Chapter 14, verses 51 and 52. "And there followed Jesus a certain young man, having a linen cloth around his naked body, and the soldiers laid hold of him. And he left the linen cloth and fled from them naked." Well, please tell me what a young man naked except for the famous linen sheet, was doing in the Garden of Gethsemene with all those apostles all night long? Discussing theology? What's baptism, anyway? People dunked in cold water to BRING THEM OUT OF SOMETHING! SO? WAKE UP!! X was among other things a catalog of early Christian headbending sex magic, not unlike the Greek Elusion Mysteries, or the Oracle of Delphi, both of which we know now used a kind of fermented russet grain that worked like LSD, and blew the mind of Socrates, among others. So help! keep the secrets! What secrets? Well, walking on water, loaves and fishes, water into wine, raising the dead, all the Christian miracles, which are plainly nothing but old fashioned magic. I mean, what else was going on in that garden? All night? Initiation into what? Jesus Christ was a homosexual magician.

HUSBAND: That's the opera the citizens of the United States are paying you to write?

MUSICIAN: Yep.

HUSBAND: Jesus Christ SuperQueer?

WIFE: Oh!

HUSBAND: Are you queer?

MUSICIAN: Gay, please. Sometimes.

WIFE: And sometimes not?

MUSICIAN: And sometimes not.

WIFE: Thank God for small favors.

HUSBAND: Do you like that photograph of a man with bull whip stuck up his ass?

MUSICIAN: Very much.

HUSBAND: Of Jesus Christ on the Cross in piss?

MUSICIAN: Very much.

WIFE: Oh, dear.

MUSICIAN: They're beautiful.

WIFE: You were right and we were wrong. It's time you left.

MUSICIAN: No, I'll have another drink. *(He pours himself a lot of Lillet.)* As long as we're talking, we might as well talk. I am one thing and you're another!

HUSBAND: Let's have it out!

MUSICIAN: By God, let's do!!

HUSBAND: Do you think I, who received from my country rewards beyond my expectation, or what I deserve, do you think I will watch YOU insult its religious beliefs, befoul its healthy sexuality, romp like a selfish child through foolish wives—

WIFE: Oh!

HUSBAND: —and then PAY you for it? Write your sacrilegious opera. It's a free country, but make your own living while you do it!

MUSICIAN: You don't hate my art because you love your country or because my life's work is immoral or sacrilegious but because it might live and you will certainly die. For all your money and all your power, it is possible that what I create will be alive when nobody remembers anything you ever did, thought or were!

HUSBAND: You insufferable little shit, five minutes ago, you self righteously assumed I was insulting Marian Anderson, Paul Robeson and the famous Jew Glen Gould, when is it perfectly reasonable to consider Ms. Anderson's distorting inner rage at what she endured, Paul Robeson lashing out with political revenge, and the fact, master composer, that some music lovers prefer the non-percussive recordings of Dinu Lipati and Giomar Novaes to hammer-handed Presbyterian Gould. AND! If I *was* a racist anti-Semite, which I am not, do you think I would let *you* see it? You bite the hand that feeds you before it gets out of its pocket, then have the gall to call yourself immortal! You have no originality of mind whatsoever. I hope you compose better than you think.

WIFE: Am I a wall? Am I a stone, the pavement, to be walked over to a a slimy swimming pool swamp of male jealousy!

MUSICIAN: Swimming pool swamp?

HUSBAND: She does the best she can.

MUSICIAN: OK.

WIFE: Both! Both! To hell with you both! Make fun of me, while you snarl at each other like hyenas! Mean Old Daddy, Nasty Little Boy, and me, Stupid Mamma! Well, I'm not so dumb. I don't hurt anyone. I don't insult anyone. I just want to play the piano for my friends. Simple pleasure in beauty, amateur or not, simple giving of joy as well as I can, as I, in my turn, hope for the joy of heaven. Which, young man, I *do* hope for, with all my being, and think *that* is what art is all about. I resent your attack on my beliefs. I have not forgotten my Episcopal father, the Christ of my childhood, or the life to come.

MUSICIAN: Life to come. Perfect. God, or whatever made us, gives you one life, and you immediately have to watch Jesus die so you can have another one. Your religion is slobbering greed. Your music is a bar of fancy soap. You hate art, you just want to OWN it! I love this country just as much as you do, and I will fight your destruction of its honesty and its soul!

HUSBAND: And we will fight, with all our power and influence, *your* corruption of the United States of America!

MUSICIAN: I will win!

WIFE AND HUSBAND: We will win!

(Enter Visitor, a man in black.)

VISITOR: Good evening.

HUSBAND: How did you get in here?

VISITOR: The door was open.

HUSBAND: No, it wasn't.

VISITOR: It was to me.

HUSBAND: Who are you?

VISITOR: A Bosendorfer. May I?

(The Visitor sits at the Bosendorfer, and plays a few bars of Bach. Wife, Husband and Musician listen, astounded. Visitor stops.)

VISITOR: Jesu, Joy of Man's Desiring. Beautiful. And a beautiful Bosendorfer. Too bad. (*The Visitor stands up.*) It was a small sea gull, no one knew why it was there, a little bigger than my hand. Faulty protection maintenance by the airline. A 707 fell out of the sky onto this house. There are no survivors.

WIFE: What?

MUSICIAN: *(Simultaneous.)* Huh?

HUSBAND: *(Simultaneous.)* I beg your pardon?

VISITOR: *(Smiling.)* Bach, Jesus, Death. Shall we go?

WIFE, HUSBAND, AND MUSICIAN: Go?

VISITOR: Now. Come along.

WIFE: My life?

HUSBAND: My money?

MUSICIAN: My opera?

    (Blackout. Marche Militaire.)

END OF PLAY

What I Meant Was

BY CRAIG LUCAS

FOR CONNIE WEINSTOCK

"...but he would have us remember most of all
to be enthusiastic over the night,
not only for the sense of wonder
it alone has to offer, but also

because it needs our love."

—W.H. Auden, *In Memory of Sigmund Freud*

CHARACTERS

HELEN: 49
J. FRED: her husband, 47
FRITZIE: their son, 17
NANA: Helen's mother, 77

Helen, J. Fred, Nana and Fritzie are at the dinner table in their suburban kitchen. All but Fritzie are frozen, reaching for plates, mid-conversation. Fritzie looks front; he wears jeans and a flannel shirt, untucked.

FRITZIE: It's 1968 and we're at the dinner table in Columbia, Maryland—about eighteen miles southwest of downtown Baltimore. Upstairs on my parents' dresser is a photograph inscribed to me from J. Edgar Hoover the year I was born. My mother has gone over the faded ink with a ballpoint pen so you can be sure to still read it. On this wall in another eight years will hang a letter to my mother from Gerald Ford, thanking her for her letter of support. Right now we're in the middle of discussing the length of my hair and the clothes I have taken to wearing. The year before this I painted my entire bedroom black. Here then is everything we meant to say.

(The others unfreeze; they calmly eat their food and affectionately address one another throughout.)

J. FRED: What I think is probably at the root of our discomfort with your favoring long hair and denim is that for your mother and me and also for Nana, because we all survived the Great Depression and in some way feel we triumphed over that—coming from the working class and from immigrant stock, and because so much effort went into that struggle...

FRITZIE: Yes.

J. FRED: ...and we know in a way that you probably never will know what it means to go hungry and to have to work with your hands...

FRITZIE: Probably not.

HELEN: Let's hope not.

J. FRED: ...it seems an affront to our values to see you purposely dressing like a hobo. For that's what denim is, the costume of laborers, the unemployed. When we have seen so many people forced into that position very much against their will.

FRITZIE: I can understand that.

HELEN: And for dad's generation and mine, the idea of protesting a war which our own government has deemed to be necessary, much less desecrating our flag or burning your draft card, again flies in the face of so much we consider essential to our being.

FRITZIE: Yes.

HELEN: I know that a time will come when we will all look back and we'll say, "Perhaps this war was ill-advised," and, "Wasn't that quaint that we were so upset about the way Fritzie dressed," and we will recognize that we were probably as upset about the fact that you were growing up and we were going to have to let you go as we were about your hair which, in the final analysis, is absurdly superficial.

J. FRED: Yes, and your mother and I were also trying to grapple, in admittedly inchoate fashion, with the subterranean knowledge that you were, and are, homosexual.

FRITZIE: I know.

HELEN: And we didn't want you to live a lonely persecuted existence which, after all, is all we were ever told about the lives of gay people.

FRITZIE: And I know, Dad, that I most likely made you feel in some way personally culpable, as if my sexual orientation were some cruel whim of fate, implicitly criticizing you for having been a special agent for the F.B.I. which did so much to help contribute to our national perception of gays as threats to society.

J. FRED: Of course, I can see now with the benefit of hindsight, and the education which you have so patiently provided, that my activities in the bureau, though they may have added further burdens to the lives of many gays already freighted with discriminatory laws and at least one whole millennium worth of religious persecution, didn't actually make you gay.

FRITZIE: No.

NANA: But you know, what I notice in all of this: Fritzie is struggling with the normal tensions and fears any adolescent would be having, regardless of his sexual orientation.

FRITZIE: Thank you, Nana.

NANA: And he is also trying, since he knows he was adopted, and now also knows that he was an abandoned baby— *(To Helen.)* And though you didn't tell him that until you felt he could assimilate the knowledge in a way that wouldn't be destructive to his sense of self-worth.

FRITZIE: And I appreciate that.

NANA: Still Fritzie is searching for an identity, and that can't be a simple matter in a family which in many ways has hidden its own identity, and even fled from its roots.

HELEN: *(To Nana.)* Yes, by converting from Judaism to Christianity, you were effectively deracinating all your offspring and their progeny as well.

FRITZIE: But I can understand why Nana wanted to do that. Growing up Jewish in the deep South at the beginning of this century can't have been easy for her; and then the subsequent scorn heaped upon her by her sisters for what they considered to be her cowardice.

HELEN: And you know Nana's brother was homosexual.

NANA: Well, we didn't call it that; we didn't call it anything back then.

HELEN: When I married your father, Uncle Julian told me he thought your dad was "gorgeous." I was terribly embarrassed, and I wish to this day I could take it back and hug him and tell him that we loved him, no matter how he made love.

NANA: But I think we've made it difficult and confusing for Fritzie at times—and at this very table—by referring to some of my relatives as "kikes."

FRITZIE: I guess it was hard for me to understand where all this animosity towards the Jews was coming from, especially from you, Dad, because you weren't hiding anything; none of your relatives are Jewish, are they?

J. FRED: No, but you know how illiterate and ignorant my mother was. Well, you didn't really.

HELEN: No, I made your father ashamed of her, because I was; she was so uneducated, uncultured. Perhaps dad thought he could distance himself from the Jew he knew I was by—

J. FRED: My mother didn't want me to marry your mom.

NANA: I had called her up and told her we were Jewish. (To Helen.) Because I didn't want to lose you. I didn't think I should be alone.

FRITZIE: (To J. Fred.) Mom's having ovarian cancer and the burden of keeping that secret from her and from me when I was eleven must have fueled some of your anger as well. You must have wondered how you were going to manage if she died, and been looking for someplace to vent that rage and fear.

J. FRED: Yes, I think I was.

FRITZIE: I can't even imagine what that was like for you.

HELEN: You know, I think in a sense I must have known it was true. That I *was* sick. Because the doctor wouldn't give me any hormones, and sex was so incredibly painful. I begged him. (To J. Fred.) I thought if I didn't give you sex, you might leave me.

FRITZIE: Maybe that's another reason why you and daddy drank so much.

HELEN: Well, Nana drank. And my father.

NANA: (To Fritzie.) Everyone. And you will, too. And take LSD and snort cocaine. And risk your life by having sex with hundreds of strangers in the dark on the broken-down and abandoned piers of New York, even after the AIDS epidemic begins. You watched us losing ourselves over cocktails and cigarettes and thought, "That's what adults do." You wanted to justify our actions, make us *good* somehow, by emulating us.

FRITZIE: I think all that's true. And Mom, I want you to know I understand that the only reason you wanted to sleep with me and would crawl into my bed until the day I left for B.U. and snuggle up against me and kiss me and breathe your liquory breath so close to my face was that you yourself were molested by your dad.

HELEN: I was.

J. FRED: We've all seen and survived terrible things.

FRITZIE: In some ways I feel, because so many of my friends have died now—

J. FRED: Well, your first *lover.*

HELEN: And your second.

NANA: And Tom is sick now, too.

FRITZIE: Well...I'm more prepared to face my own death than you'll be, Mom.

J. FRED: Well, we have thirty years before she gets lung cancer.

FRITZIE: But Nana already is senile.

(Nana nods.)

FRITZIE: And all of us are alcoholics.

HELEN AND J. FRED: Yes.

HELEN: Well, not Nana.

NANA: I'm not really. I wasn't.

(Fritzie kisses Nana on the cheek.)

FRITZIE: You were the first person I really knew who died.

J. FRED: No. My mother was the first.

FRITZIE: Oh, that's right.

J. FRED: I think you didn't say you were sorry the night we told you she was dead because I never held you or told you I loved you, and you had no idea how to relate to me emotionally.

FRITZIE: I really didn't. I didn't know what I was supposed to say. When I saw you cry at her funeral, I couldn't imagine what was wrong with you. I thought you had a foot cramp. Literally. It was so shocking—that contortion seizing your face in the middle of your walk back from the casket.

J. FRED: I do love you.

FRITZIE: I love you.

J. FRED: And I forgive you for saying it to me so often when you know how uncomfortable it makes me feel.

HELEN: *(To J. Fred.)* And I forgive you for never saying it in fifty years of marriage. For saying "Phew!" which, if you recorded it and slowed it down, might sound like "I love you." "Phew!" "I love you!" but to ordinary human ears sounds like "Phew, I didn't have to say I love you!"

J. FRED: And I forgive you for not having children, for being afraid.

HELEN: And I forgive you for not magically knowing the doctors were wrong about my kidneys being too weak, and for not being able to take that fear away, or any of my fears, because you were in some ways more afraid than I.

NANA: I forgive you all for screaming at me when I couldn't remember anything. *(To Helen.)* When I picked up the knife and tried to stab you.

HELEN: I understood.

NANA: And for putting me in the home.

FRITZIE: Mom, I'm sorry I threw the plate of pasta at you and called you a "Cunt."

HELEN: I'm sorry I said your therapy wasn't working.

FRITZIE: *(To J. Fred.)* I'm sorry I embarrassed you by doing the cha-cha in the outfield and being so disinterested in and poor at sports.

HELEN: *(To Fritzie.)* I'm sorry we didn't let you know it would be okay if you turned out to be gay.

NANA: And an atheist.

J. FRED: And a Communist.

HELEN: And I'm sorry I told you your father hated homosexuals when it was me, and it was only fear and ignorance.

FRITZIE: *(To J. Fred.)* I'm sorry I asked if I could touch your penis the only time we ever took a shower together, when I was four. I know that freaked you out.

J. FRED: *(To Helen.)* And I forgive you for getting lung cancer.

FRITZIE: I do, too.

NANA: I'll be dead by then. *(To Fritzie.)* I forgive you for calling me a racist pig when I said Martin Luther King was an uppity nigger.

FRITZIE: It's the way you were raised. *(To Helen.)* I forgive you for telling me that my career was more important than going to the hospital in Denver with Tom when he had AIDS-related tb and that was the only place he could get treatment, and for suggesting that I should let him go by himself.

HELEN: *(To Fritzie.)* I forgive you for lighting the woods on fire. And for making me feel like such a failure as a mother up until and even including this very instant.

J. FRED: *(To Fritzie.)* And I forgive you for what you and I both know you did once and I can't say, or you'll probably be sued.

FRITZIE: Thank you.

HELEN: *(To Fritzie.)* And I forgive you for trying to kill yourself and leaving that awful, long note saying your father and I were "NOT TO BLAME" over and over. I forgive you for pretending you didn't know me when I walked into the wall of plate glass at your grade school and broke my nose.

FRITZIE: I forgive you for not being the parents I wanted—articulate and literate and calm.

HELEN: People who knew how to use words like "deracinate."

J. FRED: "Inchoate."

NANA: "Emulate."

J. FRED: I forgive you for being ashamed of us, for telling us that you were going to look for your natural parents; I forgive you for never finding them and, being so horrified at whatever you found, you had to come begging our forgiveness.

HELEN: I do, too. And for telling everyone that I pushed you onto the stage and saying to Deborah Norville and Bryan Gumbol that you were gay when I asked you not to. When I said I would lose all my friends if you did.

J. FRED: Well...it was important.

FRITZIE: And you didn't. Did you? Is that why you seem so alone now?

J. FRED: No.

FRITZIE: Did I do that?

(Helen looks at him for a moment. She gently shakes her head.)

J. FRED: Love is the hardest thing in the universe. Isn't it?

(Pause.)

NANA: No.

(They stare, lost in contemplation. Fritzie gently kisses each of his parents on the cheek.)

END OF PLAY

A Backward Glance

BY JULIE McKEE

AUTHOR'S NOTE:
This play should be staged with a minimum of movement and a minimum of set.

ORIGINAL PRODUCTION
A Backward Glance was originally produced at The Ensemble Studio Theatre, May 1997. It was directed by Julie Boyd with the following cast:

Evelyn.................................Sandra Shipley
Cherry ....Stephanie Roth

PLACE
Auckland, New Zealand

TIME
Summer, 1979

CHARACTERS
EVELYN: 50. Middle class, a little eccentric, lady like, pretentious, funny, lonely, hopeful. Drinks. Covers everything with gaiety and chat. Husband left her seven years ago. Would like Cherry to re-enter her son's life to break up his impending marriage, so that things would be the way they were.

CHERRY: 26. Jewish. Wears black. A weary, world traveler returned home in the hopes of finding some roots. Cultured, graceful, probably has a bit of a dark past. Still in love with David.

New Zealand. Summer of 1979. Suburb of Auckland. Hot afternoon. An enclosed verandah with a couple of deck chairs and a cocktail cart. Two women are seated. One is about fifty, very colorfully and inappropriately-dressed for gardening, bare feet, a large sun hat draped over the back of the chair. She looks very hot. The other is about twenty-six, dressed expensively casual, totally in black and looking a bit arty. They both wear sunglasses and sip their drinks.

EVELYN: I can't get over it. I just can't get over it. I just popped my head over the hedge, and there you were. Let me get another look at you. It's been years. How long has it been? Seven?

CHERRY: Three.

EVELYN: What are you doing in this neck of the woods? You should have called. Look at me, happy feet, happy face. You know I'm on my own now?

CHERRY: Ah, yes.

EVELYN: Haven't met anyone yet you know. God I'm thirsty as anything. Clipping the hedge is thirsty work, let me tell you. How's your beer?

CHERRY: Lovely, cold thank you Mrs. Robotham. (Robottom.)

EVELYN: Call me Evelyn, you're old enough. I prefer Pimms myself.

CHERRY: What a beautiful dress.

EVELYN: Thank you.

CHERRY: I didn't used to like beer you know. But when it's so hot…

EVELYN: No I don't care for it, makes me feel a bit uncomfortable.

CHERRY: Gassy?

EVELYN: Your mother and father must be very pleased to see you again mustn't they? I mean seven years.

CHERRY: Three.

EVELYN: How are your parents?—Well your mother anyway? Keeping well is she?

CHERRY: Oh yes, mum's fine. Thank you. Yes, actually they're both fine. Thank you.

EVELYN: Oh so your father is still…

CHERRY: Yes, he's still…

EVELYN: Incarcerated. Mmm. Haven't seen your mother for ages. Used to pop by every now and then but she will keep those big dogs and they do insist on barking and growling and jumping all over me. I realize you have a lovely home and grounds to protect, but I'm afraid to get out of the car. Bottoms up. *(Evelyn drinks her Pimms down in one go and prepares another.)* Well I must say you are looking wonderful.

CHERRY: So are you.

EVELYN: And sounding so British. How long are you back for this time?

CHERRY: Oh I'm here for good now...

EVELYN: No luck then?

CHERRY: Excuse me?

EVELYN: You didn't meet Mr. Right?

CHERRY: Mr. Right?

EVELYN: You know. A nice Jewish boy.

CHERRY: Oh. No. I didn't.

EVELYN: Well that's a pity. I mean because I remember your mother telling me that there were none here. Which seemed a little odd to me at the time. I mean, I know New Zealand isn't actually teeming with Jews, but...You remember many many years ago, Mr. Robinson, the Mayor of Auckland. He was a Jew or so I heard. So I mean they are here.

CHERRY: Oh they're everywhere. And I've met them all, believe me.

EVELYN: You have?

CHERRY: None of them would suit my parents.

EVELYN: Well I think you're better off back home with a nice New Zealander. Down to earth, you know. What do you think?

CHERRY: Definitely a thought. But um...the search is still on. New York's next according to mum. It has the largest population of Jews outside Israel.

EVELYN: Fancy that.

CHERRY: Uh-huh

EVELYN: And you're not keen. Yes I can tell.

CHERRY: You see I can either try New York, a kibbutz or Sydney. None of which are really me. I mean please, an Australian? I mean unless they've traveled, what good are they? What do you think?

EVELYN: I don't know what to think. What's wrong with New York?

CHERRY: Tribal, very tribal.

EVELYN: Oh.

CHERRY: How's David?

EVELYN: You haven't seen him yet?

CHERRY: I've only been back in the country for two days.

EVELYN: Marvelous, marvelous, wonderful, just wonderful. God couldn't have given me a better son. He passed the bar naturally.

CHERRY: Naturally, three years ago, I was here.

EVELYN: Flying colors. He's got a good job. Just as well he's getting married.

(Cherry chokes.)

CHERRY: Excuse me?

EVELYN: You heard.

CHERRY: To who?

EVELYN: A lovely girl. A really lovely girl. Not as lovely as you though.. and, get this, she's going to be a lawyer just like him.

CHERRY: No.

EVELYN: Yes. He plans on making heaps and heaps of money and buying a Victorian in Remuera. (Rem-you-era.)

CHERRY: Ambitious.

EVELYN: Oh yes, yes. Well he always was ambitious. You know, I always thought that you two would…well I hoped that…well I guess it just wasn't ever going to be was it? Not in the stars as they say?

CHERRY: No.

EVELYN: No. Mind you…now this is strictly between you and me…I do, if I'm completely honest, have a few tiny, weeny, doubts about her.

CHERRY: Why?

EVELYN: I mean she's a nice girl. Her mother says that she's never been any trouble at all. A fine girl. And I'm sure she's right. But! But! It can't keep a clean kitchen, let alone a clean house. Terrible. The training that girl must have had…Now I know your mother's as neat as a pin, and she never trained you to be a slut. Second of all she doesn't even bother to iron her pillowcases and doesn't even bother to hide the fact. No. Says she's got better things to do.

CHERRY: Mmm.

EVELYN: Thirdly, she's the type of person, who after using public transport, will come right into your home and sit on your bed. I just can't stand those sort of people. But you haven't heard the worst! The worst thing of all was…cause I had to stay the night at her house, under protest of course because she thought I was too drunk to drive. Ha! I mean they're living together she and he, don't ask me, just don't ask, but that's the way everyone does it nowadays. I don't say anything, I keep my mouth shut. No-one wants my opinion anyway. So I go for dinner, you know, cooks really well, nice manners, and all that, which of course are extremely important, especially in this day and age…where was I? Oh. But!, I had to ask for two towels. Now I ask you. How did she think I was going to manage with only one towel?

CHERRY: One towel?

EVELYN: Yes. I mean to say. You've got to have one towel for the upper part of your body and one for the lower part don't you? Dirty. She's dirty. I hate to say it, but it's true. Shame really 'cos I like her. Very bright. Comes from a lovely family. Plenty of money as I said, but of course that's not everything as you well know. Oh! and you must know them, they're Jews too! I mean we hardly got through discussing how many of you there are. Father's in sacks or burlap or something or other. Fisher's the name. Marilyn Fisher.

CHERRY: Oh yes, I know her!

EVELYN: So what's your impression of her dear? Speak honestly.

CHERRY: Well a twin set and pearls sort of a girl, studious, serious...

EVELYN: In other words a bore...

CHERRY: A drip actually.

EVELYN: A drag...

CHERRY: A mouse!

EVELYN: Not his type at all!

CHERRY: No!

EVELYN: No! He usually goes for the more flamboyant type. Would you like another beer? Cocktail? Anything you like.

CHERRY: Whiskey, ice. Thanks.

EVELYN: Well you'll be here for the wedding I suppose, if you're not on a kibbutz—which I very much doubt...

CHERRY: *(Overlap.)* So when is the wedding?

EVELYN: I don't know. Nothing's official you understand. I don't know that he's even asked her yet. So there's time. Not much though, if you know what I mean. And anyway how would they get married? Where would they get married! Who would marry them? You wait till you see him. It's been years.

CHERRY: Three.

EVELYN: He's developed, come out of his shell, he used to be shy as a kid. You wouldn't know him now and so sophisticated with it. He's quite a man about town. Broken a few hearts along the way if I'm not mistaken. Going away to university really was a turning point. Well it was a turning point for all of us. How's your drink dear?

CHERRY: Fine thanks. Ah...

EVELYN: Well sing out if you want another. So tell me love, what have you been up to in London?

CHERRY: Bounced around, little bit of Europe, Amsterdam, Copenhagen...

EVELYN: Not a hippy, I hope.

CHERRY: Worked for Conde-Nast a while, reception, this and that...Do you mind if I smoke?

EVELYN: Please. *(Evelyn gets ashtray from drinks cart.)*

CHERRY: Then I got homesick for good old New Zealand if you can believe that.

EVELYN: Well I wouldn't mind having you for a daughter-in-law I can tell you that much. Only if you settle down of course. Are you feeling alright dear?

CHERRY: Yes, it's just the heart, heat I mean. Gee it's hot isn't it? Phew!

EVELYN: Would you like to go inside?

CHERRY: Oh no it's alright. Actually I should be getting along.

EVELYN: You know I'm still on my own?

CHERRY: Ah, yes.

EVELYN: David left, you left, he left. It was a tragedy. A real tragedy, for me I mean. I thought I had a good marriage. I thought I was loved. But he just looked at me one day and decided to split. Hit the road Jack, and I still haven't met anyone new. And I'm so bored...

(Cherry yawns loudly.)

EVELYN: and if you're bored, you're boring.

CHERRY: No!

EVELYN: That's what they say.

CHERRY: Oh God! I'm so sorry. Jet lag. It just popped out!

EVELYN: That's alright.

CHERRY: I've only been back two days.

EVELYN: I understand.

CHERRY: I don't feel tired. The seasonal change, culture shock...

EVELYN: I said I understand!

CHERRY: *(Pause.)* It's just that I get a bit disoriented sometimes.

EVELYN: Yes dear, we all do.

CHERRY: Perhaps you should travel.

EVELYN: No I'm disoriented enough as it is. In the old days maybe, just up and go. No, I may never come back.

CHERRY: Everyone comes back.

EVELYN: Yes yes, well look at you. Here you are. I was clipping the hedge and here you are. I thought I was hallucinating.

CHERRY: I had this incredible urge to see the old neighborhood.

EVELYN: And me I hope. Notice any changes?

CHERRY: A few.

EVELYN: A few! Your parents got out while the going was good, before anyone else even thought about it. Lucky things. *(Evelyn indicates the neighbors.)* Look around you. Look who's moved in! It's all gone downhill. I keep telling myself that I have to sell, but where would I go? This is my home.

(Evelyn sees Cherry looking at her watch.)

EVELYN: How about some lunch?

CHERRY: I really do have to be going.

EVELYN: You've led an incredible life you know. You've been all over the world.

CHERRY: Yes.

EVELYN: What have you come back for?

CHERRY: What do you mean?

EVELYN: Why are you here?

CHERRY: I told you.

EVELYN: Yes, but why?

CHERRY: I don't understand.

EVELYN: Why do you keep leaving. I don't think it's normal.

CHERRY: Well I don't think it is either. But I can't help it.

EVELYN: You don't have to do everything *they* want you know.

CHERRY: *(Agitated.)* What makes you think I'm doing everything *they* want? You don't see *me* married do you? You don't see *me* wearing a wedding ring do you? I've got to go I really do. *(Cherry gets her stuff together.)* By the way does he still do all those crazy things like hold his breath at the red light?

EVELYN: Oh Cherry.

CHERRY: Does he still wash his hands five times?

EVELYN: Oh Cherry! Twice. He washes them twice.

CHERRY: *(Vehemently.)* Where did he get that from I wonder, Evelyn?

EVELYN: Mrs. *Robotham!*

CHERRY: Mrs. Robotham. *(Pause.)* I'm sorry.

EVELYN: You and David were in love.

CHERRY: We were very young...It was the best summer of my life.

EVELYN: 1972. Do you remember I took Spanish classes that summer because I wanted to go to Spain with Mr. Robotham.

CHERRY: Yes.

EVELYN: To Ibiza, Formentera, Majorca...He went without me...David went to university. You went to Europe. *(Beat.)* You could stop him you know.

CHERRY: I wouldn't, I couldn't...I didn't come back to... *(Beat.)* I'm sorry.

EVELYN: I'm going to be fifty this year. Do you know what that means? It means I'm afraid to look in the mirror. Because every time I put my face up close to the mirror and look into my eyes, I cry. I mean I know I'm lonely. That's obvious. But why do I cry just by looking into my own eyes. Why does that make me feel so sad?

CHERRY: *(Beat.)* I don't know. But I don't think you have to be fifty to feel that sad.

(An awkward pause.)

CHERRY AND EVELYN: *(Simultaneously.)* Well I really do have to... Well it was lovely to...

EVELYN: Well...

CHERRY: Well...

EVELYN: Wait a minute I'd like to...

(Evelyn disappears into house. Cherry looks out over the garden. Evelyn reappears with some tomatoes.)

EVELYN: I'm not much of a gardener though I do try, God knows. You tend to get a bit dirty and your body aches like hell, but I'm getting very good at these. Aren't they lovely? They smell nice too. I've put them in a bag for you. Well...

(Cherry and Evelyn embrace delicately.)

EVELYN: So lovely to see you again. Don't leave it for another seven years.

CHERRY: Bye.

EVELYN: Give my regards to your mother. You're a lovely girl, don't let anyone tell you you're not, even if you are a bit pale looking, but nothing that a little New Zealand sunshine can't put right. Got to be careful of the ozone though...

(Cherry has exited.)

EVELYN: Bye.

END OF PLAY

Sparrow

BY VICKI MOONEY

TO THE VICTIMS AND SURVIVORS OF THE
OKLAHOMA CITY BOMBING, APRIL 19, 1995.

ORIGINAL PRODUCTION

Sparrow was originally produced at The Ensemble Studio Theatre, Marathon '97. It was directed by Curt Dempster with the following cast:

Merriweather Bear Den . . . . Socorro Santiago

AUTHOR'S NOTE

I would like to thank Curt Dempster, Kate Baggott, Socorro Santiago, Jamie Richards, Eliza Beckwith, Gerry Mooney, and The Ensemble Studio Theatre.

CHARACTER

MERRIWEATHER BEAR DEN: a mature woman of Cherokee descent.

TIME

April 19, 1995

PLACE

Beside a small house with a big garden on the banks of Bird Creek, Osage Co., Oklahoma

MERRIWEATHER BEAR DEN: My back yard is like a birdland Peyton Place in April. They're up there in the treetops, lookin' fancy for each other and singin' their birdie love songs—courtin', an' flirtin', and braggin' on who builds the best nests before they decide who they're gonna marry and mate with. They love to peck in my garden, too, so rich with worms and tender little shoots. Grampa taught me the trick of plantin' a mulberry tree smack in with the peaches. Birds will go straight for the berries and stay clean off your fruit. I get up with the birds, I surely do, and get right out here every mornin'.

I bring out the quilt I've slept under the night before and toss it over the clothes line to air. You want the sun to hit it 'cause sunshine kills a lot of germs, but you don't want your quilt right out in the hot sun, because that will fade your colors.

So, I air my quilt before the sun gets too high, and do my level best to keep the birds out of the garden. It's too early to pick, so there's nothin' else I can do until the dew burns off. I use the time to give thanks for the day. In my own way. I'm not much of one for church.

I had been out here for a while. I judged it to be comin' up around nine o'clock and I had started back to the house for my sun hat when all of a sudden, all the bird sounds went flat dead. I looked up to see if a hawk was flyin' over, but there wasn't no hawk. Not even a cloud. Just shock stillness.

Then, out of nowhere, this crazy little female sparrow flies straight into the screen on my kitchen window. I never seen a bird so terrified. She was beatin' her wings bloody, peckin' and pullin' at the stray wires stickin' out of the screen, squawkin' an' shrillin'. What a racket! She was tryin' to get into my house, which for a bird is downright crazy. It's a bad omen. A real bad omen. It usually means a death in the family.

For a second, I thought it was gonna be me, 'cause my heart fell heavy like ten tons of lead and my guts went all quivery on me. And that bird was still pitchin' such a hissy fit she was near flailin' herself to death against the screen, so I whipped off my apron and waved it around to shoo her off...fly away bird! Fly away! Fly away! My mouth suddenly filled with the taste of copper, and I spit and spit, but I could not get it out.

I went on in the house and latched the screen door tight. I turned the light off in the kitchen and pulled down the shade. I thought I'd make myself a cup of tea and call Doris Ray. She's the cousin who keeps the closest tabs on the family, so if something bad had happened to us, she'd be the first to know. I put on a sweater and hunkered up over my tea.

The birds were talkin' amongst themselves again, but not up to level. Definitely not up to where they were...I peeked out. When birds hug the branches in broad daylight, there is evil afoot. I decided I had to know, so I dialed up Doris Ray.

She said, "Turn on the TV, Merriweather. Turn on the TV right now!"

"What channel?", I say; she says "Any channel," and hung up. I turned it on.

Oklahoma City. A bomb. My god, I've never seen so much blood outside a war. Did somebody start a war? A day care center, they say, a truck bomb like at the World Trade Center, but this time it's Oklahoma. Oklahoma!?

Here comes a woman runnin' up to the wreckage. She's lookin' for her baby and they can't hold her. She's past one cop. Wait, mamma, wait! You can't go in there. Let the man do his job. They got her. Hang on, girl. Hang on.

It's the Federal Building, so it's gotta be political, but what a price? What are we payin' for? Oklahoma? What the hell do we have in Oklahoma that anybody wants so bad they got to blow us up?

Doris Ray called back. Her emergency/disaster unit wasn't activated to go down there, but she was on call anyway as we were expectin' bad weather. I said, "Come on Doris Ray, let's me and you go give blood. I got to do somethin' before I cry myself blind."

We pull up to the hospital, and the line was already two blocks long. Whoever did this must not have counted on us standin' up for each other like we do. We're tough damn people. Everybody whose family has been in Oklahoma more than a hundred years is descended from either Indians or outlaws, or both, and we're gonna get you, you son-of-a-bitch. We gonna kick your sorry ass.

That's all people was talkin' in the blood line, and at the Post Office, and in the bars that night. Speculations on Saddam Hussein or Khaddafi— but to me that didn't make sense 'cause Oklahomans have had good relations with the Arabs for years. Half the steak houses in the state serve taboulleh.

Somebody else said Waco because it was April nineteenth, but that didn't make sense either. Who the hell cares about some weird, gun-collectin', apocolyptic-cult, pederast who thought the world owed it to him to be a rock star? Bullshit! What kind of hero kills his own people?

The experts were sayin' Middle East, and I was thinkin': fine. Let's see how you like diggin' your dead babies from the rubble. Blood for blood. We'll bomb you all. Bomb you into oblivion, and we won't care if it's your babies, or your old people, or what.

Then, it came out that the guys were from Michigan, and I just couldn't picture wipin' out all the people in Michigan the way I could when I thought it was gonna be somebody over there in Bhaghdad. I said, "Doris Ray, I am so ashamed." She said, "Don't beat yourself up too bad, Merriweather, you just had a little kneejerk reaction." She's a paramedic, so I took her word.

Okay, you live in the free-est country in the world. You can go where you want any time you want, say what you want, live any way you want to as long as you don't hurt anybody. You hate the government? You don't want to pay taxes? Fine. Stay off the damn roads. Deliver your own goddamn letters. Dig yourself a shitter in the back yard and dig yourself a water well, too, while you're at it. See how long you last.

Well, you just can't wallow in bitterness, can you? Can't just watch TV and cry. Doris Ray came over and we tried to figure out if we knew anyone who—was in it. We didn't think we did, but it turns out that my chiropractor's niece had a job interview at the Department of Agriculture that mornin'. Some lady showed her where the bathroom was on that floor so she could give herself the once over before she went in. She made it, but the lady who showed her where to go got killed. And, Wynona Stokes, right down the road, used to babysit two little boys on her ex-husband's side who were cousins to one little girl who died in the blast. None of our blood kin was down that way.

So, Doris Ray and me, we started a blanket drive. Blankets are important to our people—her and me are both part Cherokee and blankets count for—let's call it 'security' to us,—on a lot of different levels. When a couple marries, he gives her a ham and she gives him an ear of corn and we say they join the blankets. When a couple divorces, we say they split the blanket.

I couldn't find the key to my cedar chest, so Doris Ray broke in with a nail file. She's the handiest girl with tools I ever seen. I started unpackin' and unfoldin' my quilts, and spreadin' 'em out on the bed. We're a long line of quilters in my family. It was a treasure chest full, with most every design: Double Nine Patch, Tumbling Blocks, Prairie Star, Star of Bethlehem, and a plain, big block quilt pieced by my dear old blind Uncle Bus. Grandma Ruth's quilt: Flyin' Geese, she brought from Burke County, North Carolina in 1832. Aunt Taffy's satin rosette spread—too fragile almost to be handled. A Dresden Plate, signed Leota Charles, 1907. These were family heirlooms, not mine to pass outside the family, so I decided to donate just ones I'd done myself.

Doris Ray started sweatin'. She said, "Hell, let's go to Wal-Mart and just buy some new."

I said, "No, I'm gonna pick three."

Every time I'd pick one up, she'd say: "Not that one."

I settled on the Log Cabin I pieced out of Daddy's workshirts and overalls when he died. Then, I took up the Tree of Life that reminds me so of Mamma, and put it on the pile.

The third one was my pride and joy. Fifty States. The one that has a block for each state embroidered with the official bird and flower. Real colorful, a pleasure to the eye. I took the blue ribbon at the Tulsa State Fair for it. Doris had eyes for that one, I knew she did, and she bit her lip when I put it in the box. Then she gave me a hug and said, "This will warm their hearts." I had worked every thread with love, and my spirit was strong in them all. I chanted a healing prayer over the box before I taped it up. Doris took it out to her car, and I came out back as I hadn't been in the garden for four days. I needed a good day in the garden.

The birds had took their chances on each other. They were all paired up and busy building nests. I goosed a few weeds around the tomatoes. I thought of old Nana Sims, that old girl could sure gum a tomato—gobblin' and grinnin' with the juice runnin' down her chin like a little ol' toothless baby…then, I thought of those little toothless babies, dead in Oklahoma City, who was never gonna get a chance to taste any kind of food at all, and it like to broke my heart.

I dragged the hoe on out to the squash. There I found the sparrow, dead. The ants had got to her. I got the shovel and dug a sparrow grave. Coulda done it faster with a post-hole digger, no bigger than a sparrow is, but I felt I owed her a decent burial. She was the first messenger to bring me the terrible news. I think the sky grew too thick with the souls of human beings that day, and it frightened her to death.

Now we gotta try to get over this. We're not ever gonna forget it, but we got to find a way to put ourselves back together. When they did this to us, good people came from all over to lend a hand, and our brothers and sisters who could not come, let us know they were united in thought and in deed. It happened here, and it happened to us, but we all know it could have been anybody.

In this land, we're made up of every shade, every color, every stripe.

In the morning, we all greet the same sun, and together or apart, agree or disagree, when we lie down at night, we all sleep under the same patchwork called One Nation Indivisible.

They have ripped at our heart. We pick up our thread, pull the pieces together, and we begin to mend.

THE END

Tennessee and Me

BY WILL SCHEFFER

TO TENNESSEE, WITH LOVE.

ORIGINAL PRODUCTION

Tennessee and Me was first produced at The Ensemble Studio Theatre Marathon '97. It was directed by Bob Balaban, stage manager Kim Kefgen with the following cast:

ME...................................... Joe Siravo

CHARACTERS

ME
TENNESSEE
TRUMAN CAPOTE

Theme from Gone With The Wind *plays as a large bathtub rolls onto stage.*
Me inside the tub surrounded by candles. He is mixing martinis. He speaks
with a heavy New York accent.

ME: On February 25th, 1983, at approximately 2:00 in the morning, while
taking a hot bath in his suite at the Hotel Elysee, the great playwright
and notoriously alcoholic homosexual, Tennessee Williams, died amidst
the bubbles, asphyxiated by the cap of a pill vial, lodged in his throat.

It so happens that on that same unfortunate morning about an hour
earlier, I—who at that time was a rather inarticulate male prostitute
from Bensonhurst, Brooklyn—was running naked through the lobby of
the Holiday Inn on 48th street, having just extinguished a cigarette in
the sagging white belly of a Pulitzer Prize winning poet, who had paid
me five hundred dollars to do so, but who now seemed to be suffering
from mild cardiac arrest apparently brought on by my action.

Grasping my five hundred dollars but forgoing my clothes I ran
from the hotel and lunged into a waiting taxi and throwing a one hundred dollar bill into the front seat ordered the gaping cabby to take me
to the St. Marks Baths, a popular gay bathhouse on the lower east side
that flourished in the innocent age before the plague had come to live
with us in this city of strangers.

Upon checking into the baths that night I procured for myself the
honeymoon suite. The only room in the entire place with a double bed,
and quickly finding a dealer that I frequented at this establishment,
bought for myself a variety of pills that would serve various purposes for
the time I expected to stay there. In the spa room which contained a
large and fairly clean jacuzzi, after having popped a few brightly colored
pills I attracted the attention of an attractive blonde bodied fellow with
a mustache and highly developed pectoral muscles, which had recently
come into fashion. He wore only a towel and workboots. Affecting my
most masculine demeanor, which I had perfected through years of rig-
orous conditioning, I was able to lure this paragon of manhood back to
my room. After sharing a joint, and carefully avoiding any conversation
that might break the spell, we went at satisfying our obviously mutual
desire. After approximately fifteen minutes, and at precisely 2:00 A.M.,
exactly as uptown from us Mr. Williams was choking in his tub, I began
to come.

And for a reason that till this day must remain a mystery to me—
all at once I was coming and screaming and choking and yelling: "Oh

baby, Oh baby," in a ridiculously southern accent that stuck foreignly in my throat. As I watched my new buddy stare at me with obvious discomfort, I tried to apologize for my sudden and embarrassing display, but all that came out of my mouth was a high pitched cackle, and without being able to stop myself, I heard myself say: "Oh baby that was just FABULOUS—now why don't you run on down to the corner drugstore and get me a nice lemon coke with lots of shaved ice."

My blonde friend fled screaming from the honeymoon suite and I, badly shaken, staggered to the mirror and stared in shock and horror at what I saw reflected there, for the eyes that stared back at me were not my own, and I knew somehow quite clearly, that in one shining instant, oblivious as to how and why he had chosen me, the soul of Tennessee Williams had leapt into my body like a candle flame leaping into the dark night; I was possessed.

(Tubular bells plays.)

ME: "What are you doing?"

TENN: I'm moving in baby.

ME: You can't move in. Get out of me!

TENN: But Honey—we've had this date with each other from the beginning.

ME: Why do you have to move into me?

TENN: I've come back for love, Baby…and you have the body to get it for me.

ME: I don't even know who you are!

TENN: Jus' hush up then sweetie…I've always depended on the kindness of strangers.

ME: This was indeed a predicament of major proportions for me, as I had practiced a lifetime avoiding such flagrant effeminacy. And so fleeing from the baths after obtaining some clothes I instinctively searched for the nearest Catholic Church, believing exorcism to be my only hope.

When I entered the Church of the Heavenly Mother on 3rd street it was empty, save for a rather young and attractive priest who was wearing a simple black habit and swinging a smoking incense burner over the altar. I ran to him, genuflecting at his feet. I was about to explain my unfortunate situation when Tennessee who was putting up a tremendous fight to inhabit me, lurched into high gear. And again unable to control myself, while looking the priest up and down, I intoned: "DAHLING, I love your dress but your bag's on fire." Expecting the priest to take grave offense I cringed before him. But I was surprised when I heard him let out a fluttering shriek of a laugh, and next thing I knew he had whisked me into a confessional and began to perform an unspeakable act on me with great gusto and positively religious fervor. It wasn't long before I felt myself tremble with ecstasy and again Tennessee's voice sighed unbidden from my lips: "Oh Baby—sometimes there's God—so quickly." And soon it was quite clear to me that this Tennessee Williams was planning to move in for good. I began to speak with a southern accent even as I despised his presence inside me. *(Southern Accent creeps in.)*

He dragged me to bar after bar in search of love, to all the bars I had frequented before to earn my living. Sometimes he would have me affect my most unavailable demeanor, urging me to remember that the only thing that men hated more than women were homosexuals. And on those nights, we were remarkably successful at winning the sexual favors of boys of all different colors shapes and sizes. However there were nights when Tennessee would get bored and invite Truman Capote, who was recently deceased, to join us in my body—at which times I would sit at the bar carrying on lisping conversations with myself:

TRU: But you know, Tom, that the only thing that men hate more than women are homosexuals.

TENN: Yes, baby, and the only thing that homosexuals hate more than women are themselves.

(Truman gives a thick lisping laugh.)

TENN: Please, Many. You're completely destroyin' our image as the strong silent type.

ME: But either way we played it, the elusive love that Tennessee had come back for, continued to elude us. I however became used to having Tennessee in my body. We had a strange sort of marriage, and for the first time in my life I experienced a more delicate sensibility. I became morose, I began to think about the sadness of the world. It was rather delicious. I bought a typewriter and started to write bad plays which Tennessee criticized unmercifully.

And then one night the impossible happened. We both fell in love with the same boy. A bright particular boy. Tennessee made me kiss him...right on the mouth. Something I had never done before, not even for money—because I guess I knew that it would make me a *real* homosexual. And the boy kissed back with sincerity. And I found I liked it.

The object of our mutual infatuation was Freddy, who was in all ways a delight to behold, both in appearance and personality. I suppose Freddy was a notoriously modern homosexual. Full of himself, unashamed, in your face. Beautiful. He seemed actually to contain a wholeness of qualities that might best be described as a self. And the tragedy of our love for Freddy was: that Freddy really did love us. And I think that this love was unacceptable to Tennessee and me. It was not long after that, while taking a bath, that Tennessee told me he was departing.

TENN: It's all loss here honey, and I could never bear it. Never then and never now, but thank you for the ride.

ME: Please don't leave me Tenn. I'm just street trash without you.

TENN: No you're not baby, you just need to take hold of yourself—and gently, gently with love, hand your life back to yourself.

ME: And then he was gone—flying up, up in his bathtub, and into the night. Now I live alone. But there is something of Tennessee that remains with me still. A longing, a nostalgia for a time that will never be again. I might even go so far as to say that I miss those old days. Perhaps I am walking on the streets of this city, and I pass the old location of a bar or a nightclub that we used to frequent. Or perhaps I hear a familiar strain of music, a Donna Summers song, and the memories of that time rush back upon me, like the crystalline lights of a mirrored disco ball, like a thousand pieces of broken glass—Oh Tennessee I tried to forget you. But its been harder than I ever thought it would be. For nowadays the world is lit by lightning, so blow out your candles Tennessee. And so good bye.

(Me blows out the candles around the bathtub. Blackout. Donna Summer's: "Last Dance" plays.)

END OF PLAY

Sisters

BY CHERIE VOGELSTEIN

DEDICATED TO KENNY, MICHAEL, BARRY,
AND BERT

AUTHOR'S NOTE

I have four brothers but no sister. Then I met Betty, the sister I never had, and we told each other all of our secrets. Then I wrote a lot of her secrets down and turned them into a play. Then she told me if the play were produced she would never speak to me again.

Now I'm back to not having the sister I never had.

The stands at the U.S. Open. Rita is seated; wears dirty jeans, a moth-eaten yellow sweater, baseball cap, no make-up, hair pulled mercilessly away from her face, cheap, ugly sunglasses. Behind her sits a very dapper, prissy Man who watches the match with the utmost seriousness. To create a sense of atmosphere and movement, this Man, or a second Man, will periodically push past the sisters' seats wearing different disguises. The action begins when Judy enters, loaded down with food. She wears stylish sunglasses, stylish high heels, stylish skirt and blouse, nice hair, make-up, etc. The sound of applause as Judy slides in next to Rita. Note: These sisters have a very good-natured, close relationship despite (and as evidenced by) the rough talk. Everything Rita says and does is full of energy and animus; i.e., when Rita curses, she spits out and emphasizes the curse word with a heart-felt gusto. Still, it is important to keep her real and sympathetic (no easy task). Judy is not at all intimidated by Rita, just more aware of her surroundings. Though they both claim to be depressed, there is a love of life and a great joy in complaining manifest throughout. Until the letter has been digested, the pace is fast and unsentimental.

RITA: *(As Judy enters row, not looking away from match.)* Well? Did he call?

JUDY: *(Attempt at cheer.)* Not yet! *(Indicating mountain of food.)* I got a little food—

RITA: *(Still staring at match.)* Oh thank God! *(Puts hand out.)*

JUDY: *(Sits, looks at court.)* What happened? Here— *(Hands her pretzel while watching match.)* —what'd I miss?

RITA: *(Eating pretzel, still watching match.)* Sabatini just lost the first set.

JUDY: She did?! *(Bites into pretzel, not really watching match.)* I can't believe it—

(Applause, Rita grimaces.)

RITA: She's playing like shit. She's playing like SHIT nothing goes right for me—

JUDY: *(Reciting her self-help chant.)* I AM love. I love MYSELF and I see others WITH love—

RITA: *(Half-rises in her seat, points.)* Look at that look at that she can't— *(Loud and angry.)* —SHE CAN NOT RUN!

(Applause, she shakes her head, elbows Judy.)

RITA: Come on, I have money on this— *(To court, roots menacingly.)* COME. ON!

JUDY: *(Eating cotton candy contemplatively.)* I'll just keep eating till I explode—

RITA: *(Pointing.)* I mean look at those feet—what're they, size TWENTY? and they don't... *(She follows match with her eyes.)* —they don't— *(As crowd applauds, to Sabatini, furious.)* —CAN YA TRY AND HIT A FUCKIN' BACKHAND?—UN-BE-LIEV-ABLE— *(Calmly, to Judy.)* She doesn't move.

JUDY: *(Coming out of her funk.)* She's so pretty, though.

RITA: *(Takes off glasses, looks at Judy)* So?

JUDY: *(Watching point, pointedly not turning.)* So nothing—

RITA: Uch— *(Looks through binoculars.)*

JUDY: *(Rolling her eyes, it's an old argument.)* —I'm just saying she's very pretty—

RITA: *(Still looking through binoculars, responds dispassionately, overlapping talk.)* So you want her to win cuz she's pretty?

JUDY: *(Taking binoculars, condescendingly cheerful as she looks all around.)* Well, I don't hold her looks *against* her, if that's accept— *(Settling binoculars on court.)* —WOW! she's so big in person! You think she's a lesbian?

RITA: *(Eating popcorn.)* They're all lesbians. *(Applause, she eats more.)* I should be a lesbian, ya know that? I really should.

JUDY: *(Clapping, eyes glued adoringly to Man about to pass, she says as she rises.)* Yeah...

(Man, dressed as stud, squeezes past her. Rita remains seated. He passes, Judy sits.)

JUDY: So...how're the kids?

RITA: Oh! Here! *(Enthusiastically hands her pile of cards.)* They made you all these birthday cards!

JUDY: *(Taking them.)* Aw, that is so sweet, they are SO great—

RITA: *(Fondly nodding, watching game intently, overlapping talk.)* Yeah they are the best, they are the—FUCK!

(Applause, she slaps her thigh hard.)

JUDY: *(Smelling card, shaking it.)* And David? How's my darling Dav—

RITA: *(Looking through binoculars, completely matter-of-fact.)* Impotent— *(Makes a sour face, not nasty.)* —did they give you any POPCORN with this salt? it's all SALT—

JUDY: *(Offers drink.)* Sprite?

RITA: You got Sprite?

JUDY: Yeah. Don't you—?

RITA: You know I hate Sprite.

JUDY: You hate Sprite?

RITA: You don't know that I hate— *(Shaking her head sadly.)* Look. She can't get a drop shot at center court—

(Applause.)

JUDY: She's aging—

RITA: —she's too big, she's too fucking LARGE with that—
(Rises, loud applause, Rita slams her thigh in fury.)

RITA: —MUSTACHE! *(Sits, calm, checks her watch.)* Yeah…so he's gonna meet us here—

JUDY: Who? David?

RITA: Yeah— *(Nodding portentously.)* —he wants to "talk."

JUDY: Here?

RITA: *(Watching match, still nodding.)* Probly figures I won't make a scene here— *(Cupping mouth, very loud.)* —LIKE I GIVE A SHIT— *(Applause, they clap.)*

JUDY: Well-well, what's going on? Are you—

RITA: Nothing, nothing, we had a little fight I said a few things—

JUDY: What'd you—

RITA: *(Very casual.)* Nothing, I told him he was gay—

JUDY: Aw Rita you know how he hates that, why did you say that? Why do you—

RITA: Why? Why? *(Very loud.)* BECAUSE HE WON'T FUCK ME I NEED SEX—

MAN AND JUDY: Shh!
(Applause.)

RITA: *(Quieter.)* I mean the man talks fabric to me. FABRIC! What the fuck do I know from fabric? I said buy whatever you want, just do it, make a decision—he is such a little homo, Judy, I'm telling you—

JUDY: *(Cuts her off, she's been through this before.)* Alright look: I'd rather not get involved on my birthday if you don't mind—

RITA: Why, why, he listens to you—

JUDY: Don't triangulate me, Rita—

RITA: —you'll tell him to fuck me—

JUDY: —DON'T TRIANGULATE ME I'M SUICIDAL— *(Immediately sweet as she opens card.)* —okeydokey let's see here—

RITA: *(Intently watching match, voice full of pain.)* I'm sorry but I am withering away… *(Suddenly rises, shouts.)* YES! BABY! BRING IT HOME! *(Crowd cheers.)*

JUDY: *(Removing card from envelope, she speaks to herself. Sentimental.)* A cow!

RITA: *(Back to depression, sits.)* —I'm dying here Judy I can't take it anymore— *(Heating up.)* —I CAN NOT TAKE IT—

JUDY: *(Shows picture.)* Look. Little Didi drew me a cow—

(Man dressed as fat person squeezes by, Judy doesn't move as she considers card, a little upset now.)

JUDY: Ya think she thinks of me as a cow? Old Auntie Judy the cow?

RITA: *(Rolls her eyes, to the air.)* Uch, she has to read into everything— *(Turns to Judy, very annoyed.)* She made you a CARD, Judy vainness, Judy selfishness who doesn't want to "get involved"—how can you not get involved YOU'RE MY SISTER?!

(Applause, she claps heartily.)

JUDY: *(Giving up, turns to her impatiently as she claps.)* Alright fine! What do you want me to do?

RITA: Nothing, nothing. just... *(Beat.)* ...just tell me how to...ya know...

JUDY: What?

RITA: *(Genuinely needing this.)* I don't know—BE! Just give me some...pointers.

JUDY: *(Quickly decides.)* Lithium.

RITA: No, no seriously—

(Announcement of game score in background.)

RITA: —you're a woman—I need like a...real WOMAN'S...perspective on this.

JUDY: Alright. *(Serious.)* Do you douche?

RITA: What?

JUDY: I'm just thinking...maybe it's an odor thing...

RITA: Why? Do I stink?

JUDY: *(Eating hot dog.)* No but...he won't do oral, right?

RITA: Oral?! At this point, I'd even take it up the ass—

(Applause, they clap.)

JUDY: *(Recoiling in disgust.)* Aw come on, Rita, we're at the OPEN, come on!

RITA: *(Not apologizing.)* I'm sorry but I happen to be an extremely passionate person—

JUDY: *(Closes her eyes in exhausted depression.)* Ya know what? I have to lie down—

RITA: —married to a...a stick...YARN! I am married to yarn!

JUDY: *(Eyes still closed.)* I'm feeling a cloud of despair moving in—

RITA: *(Looks at her, uncomprehending.)* Despair? What've *you* got despair about?

JUDY: *(Waving cards at her, in an angry sing-song.)* Hello! It's my birthday! Hello! I'm thirty-one! He didn't call! You have two children!

RITA: *(Imitating her sing-song.)* And a husband who won't— *(Loud.)* PENETRATE! *(Gentle.)* I'm looking for some intimacy—

(Applause, she breaks into an Arsenio Hall "Hoo hoo hoo" chant.)
MAN: *(Leans up.)* Shh!
JUDY: *(Turns back, flirtatiously.)* Sorry. *(Tosses hair, starts up.)* Alright. I should
     go check—
RITA: *(Pulling her down.)* Judy! It's been four minutes Judy sickness, Judy
     crazy—
     (Crowd applauds, Judy reluctantly sits. Rita looks through binoculars, scowling.)
RITA: He probly wants to do that marriage counseling bullshit—like I have
     time for that crap—
JUDY: *(Eating peanuts, stops suddenly.)* Oh! I think I just got my period—
RITA: —*I'll* give him some "marriage counseling"— *(She cups hands around
     her mouth, loud.)* "Fuck your wife once a year, that'll help"—
MAN: *(Leans up.)* Shh!
RITA: *(Waving Man off.)* Okay, okay— *(Confidentially.)* The last time?
JUDY: *(Eating popcorn.)* Which was when?
     (Man dressed as woman starts to pass, Judy stays seated.)
RITA: *(Eating popcorn, thinks.)* I don't know—last fall, winter?—I have it
     marked— *(Leaning around the woman to tell her.)* —but I was making
     noise, ya know, moaning? because I am alive, which offends him, it
     offends his sensibilities—
     (Applause.)
RITA: —these schmucks clap at a double fault—
JUDY: I know, I hate that—
     *(She leans up to go, Rita casually presses her against seat with an arm across
     her chest as she continues.)*
RITA: I mean he's so soft and gentle I barely know he's there but at least I'm
     getting some so I'm in heaven I'm in ecstasy and what does he say? What
     does he say? Guess what he says.
JUDY: *(Momentarily resigned to staying.)* What?
RITA: Shh.
JUDY: What?
RITA: Shh. He tells me to keep it down.
JUDY: Really.
RITA: "You make too much noise." *(Beat.)* "Be quiet." Can you believe that?
     (Loud.) Can you FUCKING believe that?
     (Applause, they clap.)
JUDY: *(Still clapping.)* That's not nice.
RITA: And then the shop is closed. "The shop is closed."
JUDY: *(Tries to rise.)* Well, maybe cuz of the kids—

RITA: *(Holding her back.)* The shop sells shit and then the shop is closed. I mean— *(Loud, emotional, rises.)* —it's torture!

MAN: *(Really annoyed.)* Please!

JUDY: *(Judy pulls Rita down, tries to comfort her.)* Ya know what? Maybe if you tried— *(Mocking herself.)* Oh what do I know, Rita? I'm the Queen of Spades, I'm Miss Haversham—

RITA: What're ya— *(Impatient, desperately eager.)* Just go on! I need to hear!

JUDY: Well why don't you…. *(This is a touchy subject.)* …why don't you get a little…sexied up, ya know?

RITA: *(Turns to her, suspicious.)* What do you mean?

JUDY: You know…a little make-up, perfume— *(Pointedly turns to her.)* — CLEAN UNDERWEAR, ya know?

RITA: What?

JUDY: *(Energized, patronizing.)* Yeah. Throw out the underpants from the eighth grade with the blood-stains and the holes and—

RITA: *(Genuinely puzzled.)* Why? *(Now angry.)* Why should I haveta—

JUDY: *(Rolls her eyes, why-do-I-bother expression.)* It's a way of seducing— *(Starts opening next card.)*

RITA: *(Watching match.)* Why should I have to SEDUCE him? He's my fuckin' husband—

JUDY: *(Judy examines card.)* Is this a pig?

RITA: *(Back to her former anger.)* I mean, does he wear make-up for me? Does he wear perfume to seduce ME?

JUDY: *(Rolls her eyes.)* Rita—

RITA: *(Loud, a little out of control.)* So then why the FUCK should I haveta— *(Loud applause, Rita claps appreciatively.)*

RITA: —NICE!

MAN: *(Leans over, no longer willing to shush them.)* Would you girls please be quiet?

RITA: What?

MAN: I'm trying to—

RITA: *(Speaks slowly, dripping disgust.)* We are not "girls," we are women *(Loud.)* —WOMEN! *(As if to a slow learner.)* You understand?

JUDY: *(Leans back to him.)* You can call me girl, that's fine— *(Man leans back, applause, announcement of score in background.)*

RITA: *(Looks at her with pure nausea.)* Uch—

JUDY: Oh please—

RITA: —you are so gross—

JUDY: —okay shut up—

RITA: —I'm one hundred percent serious now. You give women a bad name—

JUDY: *(Rolling her eyes, eating popcorn.)* —that "women" shit all the time—

RITA: —you are the reason for anti-Semitism—

JUDY: Sexism.

RITA: *(Very angry.)* Everything, you are the reason for everything—

JUDY: *(Rising.)* Fine. So don't ask my advice—
(Loud applause.)

RITA: *(Pulling her down, contrite.)* Come on, have a little compassion! I'm in hell, I'm a nun in hell!
(Applause, they clap.)

JUDY: *(Rising again, more determined.)* But you're a MARRIED nun in hell— I'm going to the bathroom!

RITA: *(Sisterly, holding her hand, all-knowing.)* Who're ya kidding? You're gonna go check that Goddamn machine again—

JUDY: *(Facing her with purpose.)* Alright look: *(Beat, with great pride.)* I am a VERY codependent person, okay? *(Matter-of-fact.)* I have no self-esteem and small tits— *(Pulling away.)* —now get off!

RITA: NO! *(Gentler.)* No— *(Pulls her down, puts arm around her, encouraging.)* —you are a smart, beautiful, funny woman—

JUDY: *(Jumps up in horror.)* Don't call me a WOMAN, I'm twenty-eight!

RITA: Thirty-one.

JUDY: Twenty-nine.

RITA: *(Pulling her down.)* Just sit down!
(Judy, resists, Rita pats her hand maternally.)

RITA: At least wait till David comes.

JUDY: *(Applause. Judy reluctantly sits back.)* Fine. *(Beat.)* Fine— *(Begins self-help chant as she struggles with next envelope.)* —I am love, I love myself— anhh, fuck it! *(Rips open envelope, reads.)* "Dear Auntie Judy, Here's a poem—"

RITA: *(Delighted, watching match.)* This is Rachel? She's so fucking brilliant— hates me—

JUDY: *(Reads.)* —here's a poem from me to you: "Auntie Judy, Auntie Judy, you're a doody, you're a doody, love Rachel, happy birthday."
(Applause, she puts card down, upset.)

JUDY: God.

RITA: What?

JUDY: "What?" I think there's a little hostility in—

RITA: What're you saying? It's a poem, she's three years old, Judy ungrateful—they made you CARDS!

JUDY: *(Almost crying.)* Oh God, I'm the old aunt, I'm the old, unmarried aunt they make cards for—

RITA: *(Waving dismissively.)* Look, you could be married in a second if you wa—

JUDY: *(Whining.)* No I could— *(Suddenly striking a sexy pose, speaking out of side of mouth, protruding chest.)* —is that guy looking at me with the vest?

RITA: No. I can't eat this anymore—
(Spits out popcorn, applause, as they clap.)

RITA: What's the score?

JUDY: *(Tossing hair, beside herself.)* I don't know, I don't know!
(She rises, almost sobbing, Rita grabs her hand.)

RITA: Judy! Wait! *(Confidential, takes a dramatic beat.)* I...I've gotta tell you something. Big.

JUDY: What?

RITA: *(Slow and dramatic.)* Last night. *(Beat.)* I told him I was having an affair.

JUDY: *(Incredulous but drawn in.)* What?! *(Sits, upset for David, beat.)* No wonder he's coming here—what'd he say?

RITA: Nothing, he was sleeping—but the point is— *(High drama, she looks all around before she speaks.)* —I'm really thinkin' about somethin'. Someone. I REALLY am. *(Waits, then impatiently commands.)* Ask who.

JUDY: *(Takes out licorice.)* Who?

RITA: *(Dramatic beat.)* Catherine.

JUDY: *(With horror.)* Catherine?! David's ex-wife Catherine?

RITA: *(Excited.)* Yes! She called Sunday— *(A revelation.)* —she's turned lesbian!

JUDY: Is that why she called?!

RITA: No, he still has her AFGHAN, he won't give her the Goddamn afghan back—I said, "David, give her the Goddamn blanket already I'll buy you a new one—" *(Shaking her head.)* —he is so attached to objects—he probably fucks the furniture while I'm away—
(Applause, they clap again without turning to match.)

RITA: —but the thing is—if I had an affair with a woman, that wouldn't count as adultery, right?

JUDY: *(Not facetious.)* Right.
(Man as old man passes, falls on Rita.)

RITA: So this way I could give him his "space" to play golf and withhold sex and decorate like he loves and everyone's—
JUDY: *(She's lost in the thought of it.)* Wow, poor David...both wives lesbians.
RITA: What does that say, huh? HUH? Exactly.
(Loud applause, she claps heartily.)
JUDY: *(Bringing some sense to the table, Judy puts cards on her lap, turns to Rita.)* Alright, Rita, look: You don't need to dress up or become a lesbian or... or wash— *(She breathes in, bracing herself.)* —ya just have to be more... feminine.
RITA: *(Looks at her with incredulity.)* "Feminine?" I need to be more— *(Casual anger, watching match.)* I'M the fuckin' bread-winner, Judy, he can suck my dick!
JUDY: *(With a gentle, sorrowful smile on her face.)* Well then...what can I say. *(Sweeps invisible crums from her skirt, rises.)* Now— *(Determined.)* —I MUST check my messa—
RITA: *(Apologetically holds her back, speaks slowly.)* No. No I'm sorry, but I can not allow you to be such a fuck-in' floormat—
JUDY: Doormat—I'M A DOORMAT! *(Sighing miserably, sits back in resignation.)* Oh, Godddddd! God... *(Defeated.)* I'm so... I'm crazy about him, Rita, I just can't help it.
RITA: *(Watching match, shaking her head, unable to comprehend.)* But why... *(Picturing Monty with disgust.)* ...with that MOUTH...with the saliva always swirling and the lisp... *(She watches volley intently now, edge of seat.)*
JUDY: I know, I know but... *(Chewing on licorice comtemplatively, about to reveal her innermost self.)* ...I always see myself through the eyes of the person looking at me, ya know? Like the people in the cave with the shadow— *(Suddenly hits Rita who has been concentrating on the match.)* —LISTEN!
RITA: What?! *(Dismissing her, continuing to watch.)* The shadow, the shadow, the people...
JUDY: *(Pacified, continues oblivious.)* Yeah. Like I'm trapped. Inside myself. But then, Monty looks at me and all of a sudden— *(Waxing rhapsodic.)* —I'm on the OUTSIDE, I can see myself, I—
RITA: *(Of course this is the reason.)* Monty has a big dick?
JUDY: *(Chewing, affectless.)* Very. *(Spreads hands to indicate.)* Very big.
RITA: I hear ya.
(Loud applause, she claps, puts arm around Judy, comforting her.)
RITA: Aw, Judy, look at us...

(Man dressed as little girl walks by.)

RITA: I mean, except for the kids—

JUDY: *(Opening next card, sighing.)* The kids, the kids— *(Looks at card sadly.)* This is a picture of a rat.

RITA: *(Totally weary now, but not unkind.)* Ya know, I'm just gonna tell 'em not to make you cards anymore I mean, you're a teacher for Christ's sake—

JUDY: *(Sighing sadly, they're both in a deep funk now, almost too tired to complain.)* That's what I am, the school teacher, the old school marm, the sweet old—God, I hate those kids.

RITA: *(Comforting her absently, depressed and dreamy.)* No, no…what you do, teaching children… *(Without energy or rancor.)* …instead of working on a trading desk, surrounded by cursing, misogynistic fuckers—

JUDY: *(Now they're both in their own worlds, Judy looks around.)* Maybe I'll meet somebody here—

RITA: —only to return home to a frigid unemployed leaf— *(Calculating to herself.)* —the most he ever made was what? Seventy-five, eighty thousand? That's grocery money, that's toy money—

JUDY: *(Without rancor.)* You're so damaged…

RITA: I'm just telling you how it is. *(Beat.)* My life SUCKS!

(Applause, they clap for awhile.)

JUDY: *(Anger beginning to come to a boil, still clapping.)* Noooo—MY. life. sucks. You— *(She points at her chest.)* —YOU are the luckiest person in the world—but it's not enough for Rita—Rita wants EVERYTHING!

RITA: *(Shocked.)* Everything? EVERYTHING? All I want is a piece of— *(Loud.)* —ASS—

MAN: *(Leans up.)* Excuse me, but this happens to be a tennis match, not pro-wrestling—

JUDY: *(She's now furious.)* He's right! Why don't ya just shut the FUCK up already, for Christ's sake?

RITA: *(Totally unaffected as well as confused by the attack.)* What do you mean?

JUDY: I mean: you make six hundred thousand a year and you won't even throw out your underwear—what does that say?

RITA: I'm thrifty—

JUDY: You go out of your way to look unattractive—

RITA: *(Eating popcorn aggressively.)* That's right—I want him to fuck me cuz he loves me, not because I'm pretty—

JUDY: *(Also with mouth full.)* You're not pretty—

RITA: I know.

JUDY: But you COULD be—

RITA: *(Enunciating with fury.)* But I don't care, Judy, I DO NOT CARE— beauty is not where the power lies—

JUDY: *(With total disdain, equal fury.)* Uch, God, she is so Barnard! Why do you have to be so BARNARD all the time?

(Applause.)

JUDY: You're DARING him to love you—you're…you're like this crazy nympho… EARTHQUAKE—

RITA: In a BAGGIE! In a LUNCH BOX!

JUDY: —so RELENTLESS, SO VORACIOUS—

RITA: YEAH! RIGHT!

JUDY: NO, NO, it's sick, it's…UNNATURAL!

RITA: *(Facing off, just as angry but calmer.)* What, my passion, that I have passion? *(She pokes her in the chest.)* Well ya know what I think? Ya wanta know what I think, DOODY?—

JUDY: *(This is an ancient fight.)* Don't you call me Doody!

RITA: —I think you're scared—scared of my passion, my success, my…my POWER— *(Loud, challenging.)* —you're just plain SCARED of it!

JUDY: *(Agreeing fiercely, rising to the challenge.)* I am! And David…David's probly afraid you'll eat his dick off!

RITA: *(Yells, distinct and slow.)* WHAT DICK?

(Cheers from crowd.)

MAN: *(Rises.)* Alright, that's it—I'm calling security—

(He goes off. Announcement in background of Sabatini winning the second set. They are oblivious, both a little shaken and afraid of where they went in the argument. Rita looks through binoculars, tries to ease the tension.)

RITA: What's the score?

JUDY: I don't know.

RITA: Anhh, what's the difference, another five hundred in the shithole, what do I care.

JUDY: *(Unhappy, indifferent.)* Five hundred dollars. Wow.

RITA: Yeah, well…anyway…so you should just be glad that asshole's not calling.

JUDY: Yeah I'm elated.

RITA: I mean ya just haveta get rid of him already, ya know? Just tell him it's over.

JUDY: Especially now he's engaged—

(Applause, she claps, leans her head against Rita's shoulder, moans softly like a puppy.)

JUDY: Ohhh Rita, what's wrong with me?

RITA: NOTHING!

JUDY: No, no—I should've just read THE RULES or SOMETHING—

RITA: *(Tired of fighting.)* Judy. Judy. Look at my life: two fantastic kids, a great husband— *(Looks at watch, worried.)*

JUDY: *(Sort of in tears.)* Oh now he's great—a minute ago, you were muff-diving with his ex-wife—

RITA: *(A patient clergywoman.)* You're bitter, it's your birthday—but the point is, I never followed ANY RULES and my husband loves me, my children love me, my sister worships me—
(She affectionately ruffles Judy's hair, Judy reflexively pats it into place. Trying to cheer her up once and for all, tender, a big sister.)

RITA: —we have box seats at the Open, perfect weather—
(Judy tosses hair, Rita says matter-of-factly.)

RITA: —would ya stop tossing your hair ya just hit me in the face—

JUDY: Sorry—

RITA: *(Puts arm around her.)* —so we should just calm down, eat our food and enjoy your fuckin', stupid birthday, alright? *(Checking for tears.)* Okay? Everything's gonna be fine.
(Applause.)

JUDY: *(Sniffling, the little sister nods in agreement.)* Okay. *(She sits up, opens card, silently resolves to cheer up.)* You're right. *(Determined.)* You're right. *(Reads.)* "Dear Judy, I am writing—"*(She stops cold, reads to herself intently, then feigns calm, applauds casually with crowd.)*

RITA: What?

JUDY: *(As she subtly tries to hide letter.)* What?

RITA: I don't know…you look weird—

JUDY: *(Smiles cheerfully.)* Do I?

RITA: *(A bit concerned for Judy.)* Yeah, yeah, you're really white allofa sudden—
(Looks for card, then laughs when she realizes.) What'd she draw a picture of a B.M. with your face or something?

JUDY: *(Attempting a laugh.)* Yeah, yeah—

RITA: *(Reaching for card.)* Let me see—

JUDY: *(Pulls it frantically away.)* Get off!

RITA: *(Genuinely concerned.)* What is with you? You're shaking—

JUDY: Oh well I'm cold— *(Starts to get up.)* —excuse me—

RITA: Ya gonna check your machine?—

JUDY: I have to urinate—

RITA: What're you, Grandpa now?—shaking and urinating—what's—?

JUDY: Nothing. *(Sits, pause. She sighs, defeated.)* Here. *(Beat, holds card up.)* It's a card from—

RITA: *(Rita snatches it, recognizes handwriting.)* Oh! It's from David— *(Impressed, nodding.)* —hunh! he remembered your birthday— *(Reads aloud, a smile on her face, she loves him and it shows.)* "Dear Judy, I am writing to you because you are a person of sensitivity and grace,"— *(Commenting good-naturedly.)* —asslicker— *(Continues reading.)* — "more sensitive than Rita or I could ever be,"— *(Commenting, with raised brows, not upset.)* —oh really? What the fuck does that mean? *(She shrugs, resumes.)*

JUDY: *(Tries to take card.)* Maybe we should—

RITA: *(Pulling it away.)* Let me see— *(Resumes reading.)* "As I am sure you are aware,"— *(Commenting with a chuckle.)* —look how he doesn't use contractions—"AS I AM SURE YOU ARE AWARE"—schmuck— *(Laughs heartily, resumes reading, starts to frown.)* "—Rita and I have not been very happy these past few years. It has just been one long, protracted battle,"— *(Commenting, still oblivious but realizes something's a little strange.)* —hey, what kindofa birthday card is this? *(Resumes.)* "It seems we are grossly mismatched— *(Commenting, wrinkling her brow in total confusion.)* —that's not true— *(Resumes.)* "It seems that I am unable to satisfy her needs— *(Shrugs.)* —that's true—

JUDY: Look. Let's not—

RITA: *(Reading.)* "—but in all fairness to me, Judy, the woman is insatiable,"— *(Beginning to start denial period, comments cheerily.)* —maybe it's me, but this seems a little inappropriate for a birthday card, don't ya think?—

JUDY: *(Very upset, pleading.)* Rita, please don't read this here—

RITA: *(Reading.)* "I have tried to be what she wants me to be, but frankly, Judy, it is a Herculean task,"— *(Commenting, now angry.)* Listen to the pompous fuck throwing around the big words—

JUDY: *(Deadly serious, quietly.)* Rita. Read it to yourself.

RITA: *(Nods, obeys. Reads. Gets serious.)* I...I don't believe this. *(Reads some more, quietly.)* Judy. I don't believe this. He's not coming here... *(Beat.)* He's...he's leaving me. *(Quiet and serious.)* Oh my God.

JUDY: I...I...

RITA: *(A shocked quiet.)* My husband is leaving me...in a birthday card. To my sister.

JUDY: I just don't believe it—

(Applause.)

RITA: *(In a semi-daze, sits, marvels quietly and slowly.)* So that's…what? he was afraid to tell me to my face?

JUDY: He can't mean this—

RITA: *(Calm, considers.)* Hmm. Well. I think he does. *(Pause, then she rises, yells to the Gods.)* MY LIFE IS OVER!

JUDY: *(Worried all hell will break loose, pulls her down.)* Rita, Rita, this can't be—

RITA: *(Almost laughing, continues to read, loud.)* And he wants YOU to tell me? He expects my SISTER to tell me the news that my faggot husband is walking out on me?

JUDY: *(Looking over her shoulder, trying to read card.)* Is he gay?

RITA: Let me check— *(She checks card.)* No, no, he's not gay he is just— *(Loses it again, rises, yells.)* —THE WORST LITTLE COCKSUCKER— *(Man dressed as Chassidic Rabbi passes.)*

RITA: Sorry.

JUDY: This must be a…a joke—
(Tries to read, they sit.)

RITA: *(Calm again, reading.)* Look— *(Pointing to card.)* —look how he ends it—"Have a happy birthday," like it's just a regular little Hallmark— *(Spits out the insults.)* —the…wimp, the little…PUSSY-WUSSY— *(Applause. Softly, mystified.)*

RITA: How could he…want to leave me?

JUDY: *(Trying to come up with something.)* He doesn't, he doesn't, he's just getting back at you—venting, like you always do—ya know, venting!

RITA: *(Deeply sad and vulnerable now.)* No, no…I don't think so.

JUDY: Well but Rita, Rita let's think about this for a second—this might be a blessing in disguise! I mean, you were so miserable—

RITA: *(Totally bewildered.)* I wasn't so miserable—oh God, Judy, God. *(Pause, tender.)* I love the little Nancy, ya know?

JUDY: I know…I know you do.

RITA: *(Sits holding the card, watches the game, back and forth, back and forth, claps with crowd.)* Well…but what am I, right? A junk bond trader, a…a part-time mother for an hour a day… *(Sighs.)* I deserve this.

JUDY: Stop it, stop it, Rita! Look: YOU wanted to leave HIM, remember? This whole match you wanted to become a lesbian, this whole match you were saying—

RITA: *(Beside herself.)* Don't you understand? Don't you know anything about me, Judy, what I am? *(Holds her stomach.)* I feel sick—

JUDY: *(Timidly offers Sprite for lack of a better thing to do.)* Sprite?

RITA: *(Back to herself for a second.)* Don't offer me that fucking Sprite!

(Applause, despondent again.)

RITA: I'm like one of these protesters, ya know?—"America sucks, America sucks,"—and then they take my citizenship away—now what, ya know?

JUDY: *(Sad and tired.)* No I don't know. No one took your citizenship away, Rita—you're the BEST!

RITA: *(Weary.)* I'm just saying that feeling...of FREEDOM where you can...I mean to have that with ANYBODY, much less a MAN, ya know?—to feel that...you can say anything, do whatever—hate him and yell and it's okay, it's safe...it's safe...it's safe... *(Broken now.)* —Oh God, Judy... *(Very softly, simple.)* ...it's never safe.

(Judy puts her arm around a curled up Rita.)

JUDY: *(Applause, patting her.)* This is just...too crazy...

(Rita bites into apple.)

RITA: I feel so... *(Impressed with apple, with raised eyebrows.)* This is delicious.

JUDY: *(Also eating candy apple, in her own world.)* So...so what're we supposed to...

RITA: *(Long pause.)* Ya know...some mornings, I look in at the kids before I leave for work and I just... *(She stops.)*

JUDY: *(Gently.)* What?

RITA: *(Not emotional.)* Cry. I just stand there and cry.

JUDY: *(Gently.)* Why?

RITA: *(Nodding.)* Because they're girls. In this world. I cry that they're girls.

(Applause, she roughly wipes away a tear.)

RITA: God.

JUDY: *(Sighs, massages Rita's shoulders as she talks, slowly seething.)* Well, GOD, Rita...God. Is a man...in this world, God is a man and...man is a God and— *(Points to court, shakily.)* —and you're...you're over the hill at twenty-three— *(Lathering up, growing increasingly crazy.)* —and you have to wear these...these shoes...these Goddamn— *(She takes shoe, begins pounding it into the chair, Rita just stands there dumbfounded.)* — fucking STILTS as you SMILE AND SMILE. IN THE SUN. WITH YOUR PERIOD. AND YOUR NOSE JOB. AND...AND—

(Man returns to row, she turns to him, completely hysterical.)

JUDY: —DON'T YOU DARE FUCKING TELL US TO BE QUIET, MOTHERFUCKER!!!

(She punches him in the nose, Rita gasps as he falls behind the row.)

JUDY: I AM SO SICK OF YOU! *(Judy looks down with fist raised, about to jump down and give him some more.)*

RITA: *(Holding her back.)* JUDY!

JUDY: *(Hyperventilating.)* WHAT?

RITA: What're you… *(Getting caught up in match, head turning back and forth.)* …what're you…
(Cheering.)
RITA: —what's the score?
JUDY: I don't know. I think they split sets.
RITA: *(As if about match.)* So it's not over. *(Staring ahead.)* It's not over.
JUDY: No.
(They lower themselves back into their seats, Rita puts her arm around Judy, after a beat or two.)
RITA: Happy…happy birthday.
JUDY: Yeah. Alright.
(She slips her arm through Rita's. They watch the match in this position, maybe eat popcorn as the lights slowly fade to black.)

THE END

Mistresses

BY MICHAEL WELLER

THE AUTHOR

Michael Weller has written over 30 plays and films. The best known are (plays): *Moonchildren, Fishing, Split, Loose Ends, Ghosts on Fire, Spoils of War* and *No Bottom*. His films include *Hair* and *Ragtime* (for Miles Forman) and Lost Angels (for Hugh Hudson).

His new comedy, *Help*, premiered at Ensemble Theatre in Cincinnati, and has gone on to productions at the Coast Playhouse in Los Angeles and the Mixed Blood Theater in Minneapolis. His play for young audiences, *Dogbrain*, completed a successful premiere at Stage One in Louisville in April-May, '96, and a new comedy, *The Heart of Art*, will be produced in New York by the Valiant Theatre Company. His play *Buying Time* premieres at the Seattle Rep in February '96.

He is currently completing a new play about a maverick auto-maker, *Momentum*, for the Seattle Rep Theatre, and a two-character play, *What the Night is For*, for himself. His screenplay of *In the Blue Light of African Dreams* (from the novel by Paul Watkins) is being produced by Zanuck (Brown and Cruise/Wagner) Productions. Chanticlear Films will produce his original screenplay, *Getting Rid of Alex*, in 1998. He will direct.

One of the most satisfying professional experiences has been working with apprentice playwrights around the country when his plays premiere in not-for-profit theaters. Several writers have gone on to wide acclaim: Sally Nemuth, Heather McDonald, Christopher Kyle, and Joe McDonough. He is a council member of The Dramatics Guild of America, and an advocate of the "L.O.R.T. Contract" to provide minimum conditions nationwide for play-wrights at all cooperating theaters. Hie lives in New York with his wife Katherine Talbert and his sons Ben and John.

AUTHOR'S NOTE

Mistresses was written as a warm-up excercise for a series of two plays I am now writing about marriages between couples of that uneasy generation who sprouted between the idealists of the late-60s/early-70s, and the more anxiety-ridden overachievers of the late-70s/early-80s. My intention was to sketch all the themes I plan to deal with in these later plays, but to do so in one compact and finely focused encounter between two married, but lost and lonely men.

ORIGINAL PRODUCTION

Mistresses was originally produced at The Ensemble Studio Theatre's Marathon '97. It was directed by Susann Brinkley with the following cast:

Sandler . . . . Roscoe Born
Spode . . . . Bob Balaban
Marshall . . . . Rob Sedgwick

CHARACTERS

Sand
Spode
Marshall

A street—a former mercantile area with young professionals renovating lofts. Part of a large dumpster intrudes from the side, spilling over with the guts of an old sweatshop. The legs and backs of several chairs stick out. Sandler, mid-30s, sits beside the dumpster in a chair he has pulled from it. He is leaning forward, elbows on knees, swiveling an unopened pack of Winstons between the thumb and middle finger of one hand, tapping one end against the opposite palm, swiveling, tapping the other, swiveling, over and over, a mindless activity that mirrors his vacant, staring face. He wears an old t-shirt and work pants, his arms are huge, his appearance weathered. Apart from the cigarette pack, he is eerily still. Spode, also mid-30s, walks by along the sidewalk and passes out of sight behind the dumpster, then re-appears, staring at the chairs sticking up. He's an intense, agitated, halting man with a fringe of hair around a growing bald spot. He wears thick glasses.

SPODE: *(Behind Sandler.)* Is this thing *(The dumpster.)* yours?

SAND: *(Half turn.)* This? *("No.")* Help yourself.

SPODE: Sandler?

SAND: *(Turns.)* Spode?!

(Sandler half rises and they shake hands awkwardly, a nervous greeting.)

SPODE: What are you doing at this end of the street?

SAND: Sitting. You 'round here somewhere?

SPODE: *(Points over audience.)* Third floor.

SAND: With the light on?

SPODE: *(Nods.)* So…who belongs to *(The dumpster.)* this?

SAND: Your end of the block, you tell me.

SPODE: Unbelievable, isn't it. Even *businesses* opening here. A hair stylist. A Buddhist Study Center down there.

SAND: With the yellow windows? What *is* that, painting your window glass *yellow?*

SPODE: So you can't see in.

SAND: You can't see out, either. What do they, just sit inside and look at yellow all day.

SPODE: It stops desire. One of 'em told me that.

SAND: Yellow stops desire? That's all it takes?

SPODE: It's a Buddhist thing, I guess.

(Both smile, mostly to themselves.)

SPODE: So these chairs are up for grabs? No one'll mind if we take one? What the hell, it's my street, right? We're pioneers here. Kind of exciting to watch the block change in front of your eyes…

SAND: *(Mordant.)* Very stimulating.

SPODE: Are you out here for (how to put it), any particular reason?
(Sandler is turning his cigarette pack, tap-tap-tap, turn, tap-tap-tap, turn...
He nods.)

SAND: How's Beck?

SPODE: Rebecca? Fine. Great. How's— *(Forgets the name.)* —your
wife, *(Remembers.)* Marty.

SAND: Marina. Mari. *(Mah-ree.) (Sandler checks his watch.)*

SPODE: Me, too. Insomnia. Gets real quiet around here.

SAND: It gets real quiet *everywhere* at 3:00 AM.

SPODE: Yeah, but especially here. A neighborhood like this. If you call it a
neighborhood when there's no neighbors. *(Chattering away.)* It *is* changing, though. Paid thirty for the loft. You bought yours, too, didn't you?
A few years we'll be sitting on a gold mine.

SAND: *(Seeing Spode's restlessness.)* Do you want to sit down?

SPODE: No shortage of chairs.
(Spode reaches up and moves chairs around.)

SAND: Is your wife awake? *(Indicates the window.)* The light?

SPODE: *(Still selecting a seat.)* She has to argue a big case next week, major
preparation. Late night's the only time she has to herself. After Danny's
asleep. After I put him to bed. Give him his bath and read him a story
and put him to bed. And wash the dinner dishes. *(He barely hears himself, so busy is he with taking down the chair he found.)*

SAND: Hard being a mom, huh?

SPODE: *(Positioning the chair.)* Oh...naw, we're, me and Becky are very equal
about all that.

SAND: *(Flat.)* Good for you!

SPODE: Actually, we kind of...we just had a little—tense moment.
(Sandler laughs.)

SPODE: Is that funny?

SAND: Aren't we a couple of prize fucking specimens.

SPODE: *(Realizes, almost relieved.)* You, too? You and Marty fought? Is that
why you're out here?

SAND: I always thought the loft was enormous—until me and Mari started
going at it.

SPODE: I hate little Dan Dan to hear. Becky doesn't care. She gets angry, she
just snaps, doesn't care who's around. A kid can't understand. It's scary.
Hell, it scares me sometimes.

(Sandler is vacant again, turning his smokes, tap-tap, turn…Spode is wondering what to say next, then:)

SAND: Can I ask you something personal?

SPODE: Like, a personal question? *(Beat.)* How personal are we talking about? *(Spode clearly doesn't want this, but he also doesn't want to be rude.)*

SAND: *(Beat.)* Do you fuck around?

(Spode, after the briefest hesitation, starts wiggling the chair experimentally under him.)

SPODE: This one's wobbly. *(Looks in dumpster.)* Have you already looked through all these? One of 'em must be—maybe the Buddhist center could use them. Maybe we should take them out and set them by the door, kind of a welcome to the neighborhood gesture. *(He sets down a folding wooden chair, sits. A moment goes by.)*

SAND: Should I withdraw my question?

SPODE: *(Uneasy.)* The thing is—I find it…you really want to get into this? Even if we knew each other really well, it's kind of…not that we're *strangers,* or anything. We *are* fellow pioneers, I suppose. We are *neighbors,* but still—

SAND: *(Simply.)* My mistress is pregnant. I just found out this afternoon. She's carrying my kid. *(Spode is reduced to baffled silence. His mind is darting round like a fish on a line, desperately seeking a way out.)*

SPODE: *(Avoiding.)* "Mistress." That sounds odd. Formal, you know. Old fashioned.

SAND: What would *you* call a woman you were sleeping with on a regular basis?

SPODE: "This woman I'm seeing? "Or use the name; Terry. Lynette. Danielle.

SAND: *(Grins.)* Well, which?

SPODE: Which what?

SAND: Which one are you seeing?

SPODE: I don't feel comfortable with this conversation, Sandler. I'm sorry, I don't feel comfortable with—If you have to talk to someone, call a friend.

SAND: At three in the morning?

SPODE: There's a bar across Center Avenue. It's open all night. If you just need to talk to someone…

SAND: I've been dry two years. A bar is not a good idea. Not tonight.

SPODE: Maybe the Buddhists…don't they know about stuff like this, problems? Aren't they like a church, you can knock any time? Maybe that's why they chose a street like this, full of people in the thick of it, buying property, renovating, striving—Certainly worth a try, ring the bell. They wouldn't *yell* at you, I don't imagine.

SAND: Relax. I've said what I needed to. Gabriella's pregnant. Thanks for listening.

SPODE: *(Beat.)* You're welcome. *(Beat.)* Have you told Marty?

SAND: "Mari."

SPODE: Have you?

SAND: Are we talking about this now? Of course I haven't told her. Have you told Becky you fuck around? .

SPODE: Why do you keep saying that? What makes you think I sleep around? *(Sandler looks at him.)*

SPODE: She'd throw me out the door if she knew. Right out.

SAND: *(Looking across he street.)* Is that her in the window?

(Spode looks up, his face expressionless. He waves. He drops his hand.)

SAND: Full moon. *(Smiles.)* Stray wolves waiting for shelter, that's us. All the books she gives me to read, but you know what? Under everything, fuck feminism, women hold the keys. We try to get in, and they either open the door, or slam it in our face.

(A moment goes by, Sandler turning, tap-tapping his Winstons.)

SPODE: Are you going to smoke those? Cause I could use one.

SAND: *(Opening the pack.)* She came to the window. Maybe she's ready to kiss and make up.

SPODE: She's not the kiss-and-make-up type. She's more the I'll-tell-you-when-it's-over-meanwhile-stay-out-of-my-way type. I'll wait'll the light goes out. Slip back inside.

SAND: Marina would take the kid, that's the problem. If I left her for Gabrielle. I love my daughter.

SPODE: She's not yours. Is she? My wife said.

SAND: I didn't *make* her. The dad's upstate serving fifteen to twenty. And Mari...some women don't want to be moms, you know. They can crank out a kid but after that—Whereas Gabriella... *(Smiles.)* My "mistress"— she was born for motherhood. One look and you know it. Soft all over, and she actually jiggles when she laughs. I tell her she reminds me of strawberry short cake. Doesn't want a thing from me, either, no demands. The baby's enough for her. *(Thinks.)* If I could take Mari's kid, move in with Gabriella, then she could have *our* kid and the four of us would live together—it would actually be best for everyone. Even Marina. Except she'd never, I don't think she'd ever...

SPODE: I hope this is not a serious idea, Sandler. You're not seriously suggesting your wife give up her child to be raised by you and your fuck-of-the-moment.

SAND: I *love* Gabriella.

SPODE: The woman you love. Your mistress.

SAND: Of course I love Mari, too, but mostly I love her kid. Which is why she married me, in part. She saw I was a good dad, which is *something*, I guess—that she cared enough to find her daughter a good dad. And marry him. The trouble is, I explain all this to myself, about Mari, about her needs as a high strung, talented artist, beautiful in ways that make men not take her *seriously* is how she explained it to me—and I get this beautiful kid out of the deal. I'm crazy about her, I'm her dad, really, and for five years it's been enough, even when Mari leaves the loft all day to go—I don't even know *what* she does all day; visits art galleries, has lunch with friends, does part time jobs...I'm just guessing...she hates when I ask where she's been. *(Sandler lights their cigarettes.)* Sometimes after a day with the kid, and we're having a really good time, she'll get home and make dinner, then she'll fly into this rage about how she has to do everything around the house, which she in fact does do sometimes, she has weeks where she gets all stormy and plays super-mom until she gets bored...But I never minded, even *questioned* our life together until Gabriella came along and—how come women have so much power to make you feel, I don't know...Loved. *Appreciated.* And the exact opposite. *(He inhales deeply and ponders his estate.)* Since Gabriella, Mari seems like a witch. And that's totally unfair of me. She never promised she'd be a good wife. Or mother. We just...fell in love, the way you do. We got married. That's an obligation. You honor your obligations. Hell, maybe I'm a bad husband, who knows. I'm a good dad, okay, but— *(Beat.)* What happens to the kid if I leave?

SPODE: Can I say something here...

SAND: *(Distant.)* I never yelled at Mari till Gabriella came along. That's not fair, either. Just cause your mistress makes you feel good about yourself...

SPODE: Okay, we're talking now. Here's my advice. Lighten up. Let this Gabriella babe have her kid, do the best you can by her, but have another affair as fast as you can, and another one after that, and the minute they get tricky, get out. Fuck around to have *fun,* there's no other reason. If it gets heavy and complicated you might as well have a second wife.

SAND: Rules to Live By?

SPODE: It's more an ideal. A goal. Like anyone, I fall short. Having a mistress takes practice. In America, anyway. In Europe you're born knowing how.

SAND: *(Chuckling.)* That's wild. I didn't really think you screwed around. I was joking before. You always struck me as this sort of knotted up city engineer type with a harpy wife.

SPODE: A pussy-whipped geek, you mean?

(Sandler laughs loudly.)

SAND: *(Nods.)* In fact.

SPODE: *(Irked.)* Well, you always struck me as a beer and poker check your brains at the door kinda guy, so there ya go.

(He went too far. Sandler's a big fellow. He turns to Spode slowly. Then he laughs.)

SAND: Fair enough.

SPODE: A night of revelations. *(Agitated.)* This Buddhist place, it's really bothering me all of a sudden. Why'd they come here? Did Buddha send a message, Front Street is a hot location to set up shop, full of restless young professionals craving inner calm?

SAND: Do you *always* have another woman on the side?

SPODE: By and large. There are gaps.

SAND: *(Genuine.)* What if one got pregnant. Or fell in love with you?

SPODE: Look, I wear a ring. They know the deal. They tend to be quite interesting ladies on the whole. Breakers of taboos. Independent. Or very screwed up. Either way, interesting. Okay, we're getting into this, right, so—between you and me, my wife is a wonderful, remarkable human being who I love with all my heart, I really do. And she loves me. And little Dan-Dan. But she doesn't basically like to be *around* us, you know? She likes us being in her life. But not *around.* She doesn't want to actually spend time with us. Or anyone, really. People. She likes to be on her own. Or in court, terrorizing her opponent. I respect that. But for me and Danny, it's kind of like living by ourselves. So I get needy sometime, and *intense...* and this look, she says I get this kind of wounded accusatory look when she wants to be alone, like I think she's failing me, us, in some way, which I *do* feel, but I know it's *my* fault that I feel that way, cause she can only be what she is, not what *I* want her to be, and with kids its suddenly for keeps, so—I screw around. And that takes care of the flesh and ego-need stuff, and here's the interesting thing—Beck is always happiest when I'm with someone else. She seems to sense less neediness I don't know, it's a real mystery, maybe she feels let off the hook, but she gets nicer, and I love her even more and we make love a *lot* more, and better when there's someone else in my life, I even fantasize being with Beck when I'm with a…"mistress." God, that's a nice word. I mean, you do your best as a man, right. God knows there must be things she's not getting from me. But that's *her* problem, right? She finds a way. *(Beat.)* It's when these women *leave* me, that's when the trouble starts. When I'm all alone again. Just me and Danny.

SAND: *(Sudden comprehension.) That's* why you're out here? You just broke—? *(Stops.)*

SPODE: Joanne. Jo. She met someone. He reminds her of me. Not as good in bed, she says. But all hers. So I have to get another lady, like real soon. I love Beck…I want to make this marriage work. Jo was the best yet…even on the phone—she'd hold the receiver against herself and— *(Beat.)* This is some conversation!

(He is fighting tears. Sandler lets him have his mood.)

SAND: Look at us out here. Them in there. It's pathetic.

SPODE: It's kind of funny, actually. *(Changing the subject.)* Can you believe anyone would throw out perfectly good chairs—

SAND: You okay?

(Spode nods. Sandler looks across the street.)

SAND: Look; your light's out. Home free.

SPODE: Yeah…

SAND: Well, good luck finding a new…

SPODE: Mistress.

SAND: *(Smiles.)* Yeah.

SPODE: You, too. Find a new lady. Only way to go.

SAND: Don't forget the chair.

(Spode stares across the street.)

SPODE: I could really use one of those. If that's okay with you.

(Sandler taps out cigarettes, gives one to Spode and they light up. He puts down the cigarette pack and the two smoke for a moment and then…Marshall enters, mid-30s, all in black, wiry and feral.)

MARSH: Sandler, what the fuck are you doing out—never mind. Those your smokes?

(Sandler hands him one. All have cigarettes in their mouths. Sandler lights them up.)

SPODE: I'm Spode.

MARSH: Yeah, I've seen you on the block. *(Handshake.)* Marshall. You mind if I join you? Let's not talk for a minute, okay? I gotta get some (Yells toward the far end of the street where he came from.) SHIT OUT OF MY HEAD!!!

(Marshall paces. All smoke. Sandler and Spode exchange a look of understanding. Sandler lets out a howl, smiling to himself. Spode looks at him and understands. Sandler howls louder. Spode joins in. Marshall looks at them as if they're both nuts, but when they continue howling, it starts to feel sort of right and so he starts howling, too. And there they sit, howling away as…the lights dim. And they keep smoking, three guys outside at 3:00 in the morning.)

END OF PLAY

Real Real Gone

BY MICHAEL LOUIS WELLS

FOR F. DEAN, H. LOUIS, AND RAYNOR C.
TO THE DA'S.

THE AUTHOR
Michael Louis Wells is the author of *Real Real Gone* and it's companion piece, *Gary Christmas*. Other plays include: *Seven Pages Unsigned, District of Columbia, Fourth Time Around, Video Guy,* and *Fifth Floor Walk-up:* a trilogy of short lays consisting of *Friends?, Hermit of Ninth Avenue* and *Same Difference.* Also a musician and songwriter, he has over fifty titles registered with ASCAP and has released two albums: *Moving on to Solids,* and *Thanks for All the Lemons,* with his band, Uncle. A member of EST and The Dramatist's Guild, Mr. Wells lives in New York City.

AUTHOR'S NOTE
For the actors: the use of ellipses is generally meant to illustrate the interruption, over-lapping, and completion of each other's thoughts endemic in conversation between very close friends. Rarely does it indicate a pause. It's best played fairly rapidly. The use of colloquial or phoentic spellings ("whaddya," "yer," etc.) is *not* intended to suggest any sort of accent or regionalism—least of all "Noo Yawk." It's only meant to approximate casual so-called American Stage Standard speech a bit *sub*-standard. Have fun.

ORIGINAL PRODUCTION
Real Real Gone was first produced by the Ensemble Studio Theatre in New York. It opened on May 21, 1997 and was directed by Jamie Richards, with the following cast:

Mitchell . . . . Thomas McHugh
Karl . . . . Joseph Lyle Taylor

CHARACTERS
KARL
MITCHELL

PLACE
A secluded spot in an old family cemetery.

TIME
January, the present.

A secluded spot in an old family cemetery on the lower lower east side. Basically abandoned and overgrown, it is distinguished by ornate and somewhat Gothic architecture and, incongruously, a freshly dug grave. At rise, we discover Mitchell, a well-dressed man in his late twenties, standing near the burial mound, methodically trimming his nails with his teeth. He spits out a clipping and exhales heavily, looking skyward. He slowly rubs his eyes with his right hand and then examines his watch. He looks down at the black leather bookbag at his feet. Suddenly, he seems to hear something. He stands quite still and slowly closes his eyes, transfixed by something. His body sways slightly. In a moment, Karl, thirty—dressed in work clothes and a tattered blonde wool overcoat—appears at the gate. He enters quietly.

KARL: Boo!

MITCHELL: Gaaaah!

KARL: Sorry, man. *(Beat.)* You okay?

MITCHELL: No. I dunno. *(Beat.)* Never do that to me again.

KARL: Whaddya mean by never?

MITCHELL: You...*fucker!*

KARL: Got ya didn't I?

MITCHELL: Man...!

KARL: Got ya. *(Beat.)* So, whaddya think?

MITCHELL: Huh?

KARL: Look around.

MITCHELL: Oh.

KARL: Ya lookin'?

MITCHELL: Wrought iron.

KARL: Right. Kinda Gothic...

MITCHELL: Yeah!

KARL: Kinda right up yers!

MITCHELL: Wow. Like yer in another...

KARL: s'transporting.

MITCHELL: ...*time,* yeah!

KARL: Well, ya gotta get outta it...

BOTH: ...to get *to* it.

MITCHELL: Yeah. Great. And the...

KARL: ...burial.

MITCHELL: Oh, yeah!

KARL: It's key.

MITCHELL: Right. It's...

KARL: Active.

MITCHELL: Yeah.

KARL: It brings ya *here.*

MITCHELL: It looks fresh.

KARL: Fresh this morning.

MITCHELL: 'Cause the rest of the place...

KARL: s'in disuse.

MITCHELL: ...it's old, yeah.

KARL: Check out some of the dates over there.

MITCHELL: Uh-huh...

KARL: It's all one family.

MITCHELL: Wow. So—this *morning...*

KARL: Who knows? Some old geezer decided he'd get in touch with his roots, like literally.

MITCHELL: But how did you...

KARL: Had a call out to Gus.

MITCHELL: Gus. The gravedancer dude!

KARL: He's a good scout.

MITCHELL: He's the one tipped you to that underground...

KARL: ...catacomb...

MITCHELL: ...like deal the year we did

KARL: ...the mausoleum...

MITCHELL: ...up Fort Tryon Park.

KARL: Which was...

MITCHELL: Great!

KARL: ...but I wanted to be outside this year.

MITCHELL: Yeah, well, this is... great job, man!

KARL: It's good.

MITCHELL: It's the best one, yet.

KARL: Thanks. *(Beat.)* Five years.

MITCHELL: Yeah. Five...five...fuck. Karl?

KARL: Yeah?

MITCHELL: I forgot the flask.

KARL: What?

MITCHELL: My dad's flask. I can't find it.

KARL: Mitchell...

MITCHELL: I looked all morning...

KARL: Mitchell...

MITCHELL: Ya know? But I just...

KARL: Mitchell.

MITCHELL: …can't find it anywhere!

KARL: You don't have the flask.

MITCHELL: I know. I'm sorry.

KARL: It's okay.

MITCHELL: I'm sorry.

KARL: *(Pulling a very old looking silver whiskey flask from his back pocket.)* I have the flask!

MITCHELL: Oh.

KARL: I've had the flask for years. You were always afraid you'd lose it. So, you gave it to me to hang on to and break out on The Day.

MITCHELL: I knew that.

KARL: Yeah.

MITCHELL: It's jitters.

KARL: I know.

MITCHELL: Jitters for The Day.

KARL: The Day…

MITCHELL: …the Da's passed away.

KARL: Yers and mine…

MITCHELL: …on the…

BOTH: Very same day.

MITCHELL: Today is…

BOTH: The Day the Da's passed away.

KARL: *Very* tight. *(Beat.)* Trouble findin' the place?

MITCHELL: Naw.

KARL: Directions alright?

MITCHELL: Fine.

KARL: So, ya got my message okay?

MITCHELL: Yeah…

KARL: 'Cause I didn't know.

MITCHELL: Yeah, I been…

KARL: You ain't been *around.*

MITCHELL: You shaved off yer…

KARL: I did.

MITCHELL: Yeah.

KARL: s'in the way.

MITCHELL: What?

KARL: Sittin' and drinkin' and lookin' into the big Guinness mirror over the bar at O'Donnell's—wishin' I'd have somethin' to say to me. It was in the way.

MITCHELL: The beard was.

KARL: Yeah. And I don't want anything to come between me and the words, now. I gotta *get to the words.* So, zip-zip.

MITCHELL: Looks good.

KARL: Thanks.

MITCHELL: So, I take it yer off the wagon?

KARL: Yeah, I guess. To Drink Or Not To Drink.

MITCHELL: That is the question.

KARL: Yup. You?

MITCHELL: Well, I'm tryin'...

KARL: Uh-huh.

MITCHELL: To, ya know, pass by the open arms of my local and keep walkin', but...

KARL: What?

MITCHELL: Oh, you know the routine: "Hey, it's social and all..."

KARL: *(Nodding.) Social.*

MITCHELL: And I never miss an appointment or fuck up my job. I'm ridiculously dependable. But I inevitably awake with this feeling of remorse and self-hatred that gives the lie to the whole fantasy that I'm somehow medicating myself and that it's all perfectly alright. Perfectly in control.

KARL: That is so...

MITCHELL: Huh?

KARL: Right on.

MITCHELL: Yeah, well, ya know...? It's like I need to be *restrained.* Like with...

KARL: Handcuffs.

MITCHELL: Handcuffs! Yeah! And maybe some manacles would be a good idea, too!
    (They fall silent. Beat.)

MITCHELL: Beer?

KARL: Sure. *(Mitchell pulls a cold one out of his bookbag and hands another to Karl.)*

KARL: Thanks.

MITCHELL: Yeah. Did you see him, Christmas?

KARL: Yeah, left a bottle of Tullamore Dew on his headstone.

MITCHELL: Ed musta loved that!

KARL: Fuck Ed.

MITCHELL: Did he...?

KARL: What?

MITCHELL: ...turn up?

KARL: My brother?

MITCHELL: Ed, yeah.

KARL: He left his scent.

MITCHELL: Huh?

KARL: ...little Marine corp flags all around the plot.

MITCHELL: Charming.

KARL: Which has got...right?...nothing to do with Pop. It's all about...

MITCHELL: Yeah. *(Beat.)* Oh, I brought ya one.

KARL: A relic?

MITCHELL: Yeah. Lookin' for the flask this morning, I found it.

KARL: Uh-huh.

MITCHELL: And I remember that morning when he...when Dad...

KARL: Passed.

MITCHELL: When I got the call, yeah. I flew right out. I get there. Everybody's milling around like some old episode of *Columbo.* I need to be alone.

KARL: Right.

MITCHELL: I go upstairs and hide out in his room. I start lookin' at stuff. It hasn't hit me yet.

KARL: What stuff?

MITCHELL: Just all his stuff I'm lookin' at. And slung over a chair is this check-ered shirt he liked to wear. It still smelled like him. I never thoughta that before—how he smelled. I felt somethin' up here in the chest pocket. It was one of those little crossword puzzles. I looked at it and I just com-pletely lost it sitting there on his bed.

KARL: Crossword puzzle?

MITCHELL: Yeah, he was like a maniac for crossword puzzles. My mom hadta *ban* 'em. When he got re-married, Mary-Maria started buyin' him like crossword *everything.* Placemats, toilet paper, calendars...And that's what this was. Is. One of those little calendar crosswords.
(Mitchell has pulled the crossword out of his pocket. He hands it to Karl, who studies it intently.)

KARL: Wow.
(Mitchell suddenly starts wandering around the graveyard, calling over his shoulder.)

MITCHELL: It musta been a hard one, too. 'Cause it was from Labor Day. And it's all filled in. It's done. Yeah...

KARL: You okay?

MITCHELL: Karl?

KARL: Yeah?

MITCHELL: I dunno if I can do this today.

KARL: Huh?

MITCHELL: ...I don't think I'm up for it.

KARL: Mitch...

MITCHELL: I'm just not.

KARL: MITCHELL.

MITCHELL: What?

KARL: You know you gotta do this. *It's The Day!* You gotta go there. You gotta tell me. I gotta tell you. Then we'll drink some forty-year old to the Da's and we'll feel a lot better.

MITCHELL: I dunno...

KARL: And besides...

MITCHELL: What?

KARL: You *always* do this.

MITCHELL: Oh, fuck you!

KARL: Pardon?

MITCHELL: How do you know what I *always* do?!

KARL: *How* do I?

MITCHELL: Yeah?!

KARL: How do I know?

MITCHELL: Yeah?!

KARL: I know because every year about this time you drop off the map for a coupla weeks and it's impossible trying to find you. Then, when you finally show up on The Day, yer so twigged out it takes an hour to get you back here with me. It always happens. And it's a drag. That's how I know.

MITCHELL: Fuck!

KARL: Am I wrong?

MITCHELL: Just...

KARL: What?

MITCHELL: Reducing me to some amusing, easy-to-explain comic book character...

KARL: That's not...

MITCHELL: Like I'm not for real. Like I'm not actually happening in front of yer...Like Kendra tellin' me, all blasé and oblivious, that it's all because of my fucking star sign! That because I'm a Taurus I'm *like* this! I reject that!!

KARL: *(Beat.)* You've been talking to Kendra?

MITCHELL: *(Beat.)* Do I disappoint you?

KARL: No, but it explains a lot.

MITCHELL: This is the worst time of year.

KARL: I wish you could see, Mitchell...

MITCHELL: What?

KARL: How she manipulates you.

MITCHELL: Fuck.

KARL: It is not subtle.

MITCHELL: I stayed...I was stayin' away.

KARL: You were gettin' over it.

MITCHELL: Then the day before I drove home, she came up to me at the Christmas party...

KARL: At Max's.

MITCHELL: Yeah.

KARL: I saw this whole thing happen.

MITCHELL: And it just got planted like a...

KARL: Poison.

MITCHELL: ...egg in my head.

KARL: Right.

MITCHELL: I get home and it's like...what am I *doin'* here? Me and Marcus—Simon doesn't even show up—and we're too old for this! We're supposed to have our own families by now. Visiting the in-laws and having some horrific fight all the way home in the car!

KARL: Yeah. We are missing out on that score.

MITCHELL: Then it's all over. I'm *stranded!* I can't sleep. I need to *connect* to something. I call her.

KARL: Right. Fuck.

MITCHELL: And I'm thinkin' about her drivin' back from Wisconsin for sixteen hours and it's like exactly what I'm doing—going in reverse over all this ground I covered getting to a less insane place and...

KARL: What?

MITCHELL: I can't even tell you, man. I'm so ashamed of myself.

KARL: C'mon.

MITCHELL: I'm so stupid. I meet up with her and I'm like *pouring* out all this stuff, and she just looks at me with this look and...

KARL: Yeah?

MITCHELL: Of course she doesn't wanna get back with me. She just wants to know...

KARL: What?

MITCHELL: Who knows? That I still want her. That I'm still *talking* to her. And, ya know...why? She's got nothin' to offer like even a friend would do. We get the check, I make it outside, and then I'm just standing there in the street like an idiot, crying.

KARL: Mitchell...

MITCHELL: And I know you think I always do this—leavin a trail of blood, all torn-up over some girl givin' me the treatment—but can't you see that even if I do...even if I do, I still feel it and it's for real. Isn't it supposed to be? I'm not wrong! And I can't believe that she could just stand there...and just...stand there and not...nothing. I couldn't...not *move* her! *(Beat.)* I'm so stupid.

KARL: Mitchell...

MITCHELL: So stupid...

KARL: Mitch, buddy—listen...Ya know, I think...c'mere. *(Karl pops a beer from the bookbag and hands another to Mitchell.)* Once, and this is a long time ago, when I was a kid, my dad decided—why I don't know...I think we may've just buried the last of my goldfish. Linc, I think—I named 'em, all three, after the characters on *The Mod Squad.* Yeah, that's it! Linc had just croaked and Pop had buried him—or so he told me, I didn't actually see him do it—in the backyard. So I was grieving, ya know! And he had the idea, Pop did, that it might cheer me up if we went to the shelter and picked up a dog. Adopt a dog, right? So, we drive on down and the lady there takes us into this room where there's like this pen fulla dogs. Pop says for me to pick one of 'em. And they're all jumpin' around barkin'—big ones, little ones, in a big scrum. All of a sudden...all of a sudden I spot this one—a beagle-lookin' one—all black and cowering in the corner. Naturally, I look past all the happy, bouncing, *normal* dogs and my heart, ya know, just goes out to this one. The Underdog. He's just sad and shy and no one's ever gonna pick him, I think he thinks...So, I will. I do. I pick him. We take him home and name him Snoopy, of course. And it is a complete disaster. This dog is a miserable dog. Truly disturbed. Growling incessantly. Biting everyone. And shitting everywhere. I mean everywhere. On everything. My whole family is furious with me! Finally, Pop convinces me that Snoopy is seriously sick with some doggy mental-illness and must go to the vet. He does. And he never returns. Then Pop lets Ed pick out the new dog. He does. A perfectly sweet, well adjusted mutt—a pleasure for the whole family—and names her "Honey." Good job. Ed's good at that sorta thing. I, however...it takes me years to shake my affinity for this type of mate. *Years.* Ya see?

MITCHELL: Yer not wild about dogs?

KARL: Yeah, well...yeah. But I mean...it's harder than anything to break yerself from behavior that ultimately destroys you. And I know you tried. And I'm not sayin' that it doesn't hurt like hell. But you really gotta knock it off! You shoulda stopped with her a *long* time ago! Kendra is exactly like some...

MITCHELL: Dog?

KARL: Yeah. She's exactly like some miserable, always disagreeable dog, snarling and shitting everywhere.

MITCHELL: Yer not too crazy about her.

KARL: She took you away and she made you miserable. She's never gonna be able to help you! She doesn't wanna be happy, maybe. And she resents you for trying! So, I want you to resolve.

MITCHELL: Resolve?

KARL: Yeah, like I'm gonna do today.

MITCHELL: What?

KARL: I resolve to use my mind. I wanna use my mind for something more than dreaming up ever-more sordid scenarios to masturbate by.

MITCHELL: Uh-huh.

KARL: And you are not *stupid!*

MITCHELL: I don't feel too brilliant.

KARL: Willya call me for godsake?!

MITCHELL: What?

KARL: Instead of giving generously to the clueless, willya call me?! I don't want you dead or disappearing into some black hole. You—the only person I can really talk to at all! I mean it! I don't!

MITCHELL: Yeah.

KARL: So, ya got me?

MITCHELL: Yeah...

KARL: Are you here, now?

(Karl has grabbed Mitchell by his jacket and is looking into his face. Mitchell's eyes have closed, his face gone blank. When he opens his eyes again he seems distant. When he finally speaks, it's in Latin.)

MITCHELL: Hic et ubique.

KARL: *(Letting go of him.)* You just feel that?

(Mitchell falls forward. Karl catches him.)

MITCHELL: I'm gettin' all…

KARL: It's happening.

MITCHELL: Don't let me hit my head, alright?

KARL: Yer in good hands.

MITCHELL: Hic et ubique.

KARL: I'm with ya.

(Mitchell's breathing becomes heavy and rhythmic. His eyes are closed and his head sways slightly to some sound only he seems to hear. He seems to be humming very lightly along. Gradually he becomes quiet, silent, and still.)

MITCHELL: I won't deserve my only dream.

KARL: What?

MITCHELL: It is a hard thing to speak the truth. I am not lying. Lying is not found in my speech. I am no liar. I saw it myself.

KARL: Saw what?

MITCHELL: The sky is full of naked beings rushing through the air. Naked people are…Naked men and naked women are rushing along and raising blizzards. Raising gales! *(Beat.)* Who are you?

KARL: Mitchell?

MITCHELL: Who are those two whose faces are strange? *(Beat.)* It is known to you.

KARL: What?

MITCHELL: It is known. And a violence there that may attend it. Find within this that you seek and take heart. For it is known. It is known to you. As for the rest, only your dogs are infested.

KARL: What?

MITCHELL: The thought that The Great Summer was coming drove away all cares. *(Beat.)* Hic et ubique. *(Mitchell begins to shiver. After a moment his eyes open wide. He speaks in his own voice.)* Karl?

KARL: I'm here.

MITCHELL: I can't see. I can't see anything.

KARL: Mitchell…

MITCHELL: Are my eyes open or…?

KARL: Yeah.

MITCHELL: I can't see.

KARL: Are you still…?

MITCHELL: What?

KARL: Are you…?

MITCHELL: Shh! I'm…huh? Hearing…I'm…the sun?

KARL: Sun?

MITCHELL: Sh!! No. No, *his son*…His son…and tell him…Tell him what?
  (Mitchell starts coughing.)
KARL: Alright?
MITCHELL: Fuck. I'm losing…hear me?
  *(A violent coughing spasm ensues. Mitchell tries to stand and follow the voice
  he hears leaving him. He staggers and falls. His legs are numb. Karl catches
  him.)*
KARL: C'mere!
MITCHELL: I gotta…
KARL: Sit down.
MITCHELL: *(Tearing off his jacket.)* I'm burnin'…
KARL: C'mere.
MITCHELL: Burnin' up.
KARL: Drink.
  *(Karl retrieves Mitchell's beer and puts the can to his lips. Mitchell drinks.
  He catches his breath. Finally he opens his eyes. He squints as if emerging
  from a dark room.)*
MITCHELL: Ow! Shit!
KARL: Okay?
MITCHELL: S'bright!
KARL: Ya okay?
MITCHELL: Yeah. *(Beat.)* Did I…?
KARL: Yeah. For a minute.
MITCHELL: What…?
KARL: What was it?
MITCHELL: Yeah.
KARL: I dunno. Latin, I think. Something…
MITCHELL: *Latin?*
KARL: I think. And something else.
MITCHELL: That is *too* weird.
KARL: Definitely not one I've heard before.
MITCHELL: A new one?
KARL: Yeah, and some other stuff in there, too.
MITCHELL: What stuff?
KARL: I dunno. Like something personal.
MITCHELL: Whaddya mean?
KARL: I dunno. I dunno.
MITCHELL: My throat's sore.
KARL: Do ya think yer?

MITCHELL: What?

KARL: Ya know...?

MITCHELL: Finished?

KARL: Yeah.

MITCHELL: I dunno. For now I am. For now.

KARL: It's weird.

MITCHELL: *Tell* me about it!

KARL: No, I mean, I think this one—this place, ya know? It's like you were pickin' up...

MITCHELL: I don't know that.

KARL: What?

MITCHELL: That I'm "picking up" anything.

KARL: I know. It just seems like...

MITCHELL: Let's not...

KARL: Ya know?

MITCHELL: ...continue with the post-game analysis.

KARL: I'm just...

MITCHELL: Okay? *(Beat.)* Don't look at me. *(Beat.)* I can't think about it.

KARL: Why...?

MITCHELL: Because it makes me feel like a leper. I don't...

KARL: Yer not a leper.

MITCHELL: ...understand how it works...

KARL: Yer a shaman.

MITCHELL: ...when it does, and I have lots of bad memories coming to with some crowd standing over me, examining me like an insect!

KARL: Do I do that?

MITCHELL: No, but...

KARL: That was when you were like four...

MITCHELL: I was six.

KARL: It's not now.

MITCHELL: It scares me, okay? That feeling doesn't get grown out of. *(Beat.)* It'll go away.

KARL: Like a virus?

MITCHELL: It did before. I made it go away.

KARL: For awhile.

MITCHELL: For a long time.

KARL: You were in remission.

MITCHELL: Kids do weird things.

KARL: Kids are closer.

MITCHELL: Huh?

KARL: Kids are—to whatever it is we come from that science can't explain.

MITCHELL: Don't get all mystical on me.

KARL: I think it's true.

MITCHELL: Kids do weird things. Marcus used to bang his head on things 'til he passed out. Simon used to chew lumber.

KARL: *Lumber?*

MITCHELL: Like he was a beaver or something. Once he gnawed through most of a porch railing on the side patio.

KARL: What?!

MITCHELL: My parents were terrified. The three of us! Like we arrived via *The Village of the Damned.* But things eventually calmed down and we got on with our typical lousy Middle-American childhoods.

KARL: How…

MITCHELL: Kids do weird things.

KARL: How do you explain this *now.*

MITCHELL: I don't…

KARL: The one you had the night before he…the premonition.

MITCHELL: I don't…

KARL: And every year now on The Day?

MITCHELL: I don't. I'm not explaining. I can't. That's what I've been telling you all along. It comes out. Stuff is coming out. My stuffing!

KARL: Don't you…?

MITCHELL: The return of this weirdness…I can't even go there! It's too over-whelming I can't! I gotta start small. I gotta start with what's *here.* If I could just…Do you know about elephants?

KARL: Elephants?

MITCHELL: Yeah.

KARL: Whaddabout them?

MITCHELL: How they musk?

KARL: Must what?

MITCHELL: No. How they *musk.* With a "k."

KARL: Musk.

MITCHELL: Yeah.

KARL: Like the speed-stick fragrance.

MITCHELL: When they musk it's like they're in heat, basically. And I look to the animal kingdom now for answers.

KARL: Uh-huh.

MITCHELL: Male elephants have gotten it down to this one intense coupla month period annually where they mate.

KARL: They musk.

MITCHELL: Right. They "get-it-on" and then they get on with it. The rest of the year…

KARL: They can't be bothered.

MITCHELL: I envy that.

KARL: Mitchell, sex is a life-force.

MITCHELL: It's a force, alright.

KARL: It is. And it's not a bad thing. It is THE life-force.

MITCHELL: Where'd'ya read that? *Hustler?*

KARL: No, I heard it on *Nature*. But no one hadta tell me this.

MITCHELL: Yer tellin' *me.*

KARL: Ya just one day, ya know—*boom.* Discover them.

MITCHELL: Who?

KARL: Girls. Whodya think?

MITCHELL: Oh.

KARL: You got another one?

(Mitchell goes for another beer.)

MITCHELL: Here.

KARL: Thanks. Do you remember when you did?

MITCHELL: What? Go "boom"?

KARL: Discover them, yeah?

MITCHELL: In a magazine.

KARL: Like a *Playboy* or something?

MITCHELL: Some older kids on my block were holed up inna garage chargin' a nickel a peak.

KARL: Shrewd.

MITCHELL: I hand over a dime for me and Bobby Brayer. He goes first. Then it's my turn.

KARL: Uh-huh.

MITCHELL: They open it up and I'm starin' at this naked woman. Starin' at her breasts and I just start laughing.

KARL: Laughing?

MITCHELL: Yeah, like completely outta control. And that was the first time.

KARL: And then what happened?

MITCHELL: Uh…Bobby lured me into the sandbox; where he beat me up while the others laughed and spit in my face 'til I cried and ran home. Why do you ask?

KARL: No reason.

MITCHELL: Next day, he told me they paid him a quarter. So, I said he was still my friend, seein' as how they *paid* him and all. It was just a *job*. So, that was okay. *(Beat.)* I'm pretty fucked up.

KARL: Well, ya certainly got off to a terrific start.

MITCHELL: I was just a kid.

KARL: That what ya learn, tho'.

MITCHELL: What?

KARL: That's what you think'll happen to you if you respond the wrong way—someone'll haul off and slug ya!

MITCHELL: Maybe.

KARL: s'true. It's yer major contradiction.

MITCHELL: Oh, how I love this!

KARL: What?

MITCHELL: When you start analyzing me.

KARL: What ultimately guides your actions?

MITCHELL: Those little fortunes at the bottom of the wrapper of my daily "Bazooka Joe".

KARL: Don't fuck with me. It's what you feel, right?

MITCHELL: What I feel?

KARL: Yer gut, yeah. You go with yer gut. Even if you think it's weird—that's what you trust.

MITCHELL: Well, we'll have to stop now.

KARL: But at the same time you have this over-riding fear that every choice you make vis-a-vis anyone…

MITCHELL: Vis-a-vis?

KARL: …anyone yer *with* may have severe repercussions.

MITCHELL: You listen to way too much Public Radio.

KARL: What would be so wrong, if you felt it, to take a swing at somebody?

MITCHELL: Why does…?

KARL: I can take it.

MITCHELL: …everybody want me to have some fight with them?!

KARL: Everybody?

MITCHELL: It reeks of competition!

KARL: Who's competing with you?

MITCHELL: You are.

KARL: Competing?

MITCHELL: Probably like you do with Ed.

KARL: Like…?

MITCHELL: With yer brother.

KARL: I...

MITCHELL: You compete. You do. That's yer compulsion. Guys do that.

KARL: *Guys* do?

MITCHELL: That's right.

KARL: And what are you, then?

MITCHELL: Can you hear how rapidly this descends into juvenalia?

KARL: Are you tellin' me yer not competitive?

MITCHELL: No, I'm tellin' ya I got it full-blown. It's like the most tangible evidence inside me I can describe as evil.

KARL: To you then, competition is on a par with real evil?

MITCHELL: It's the ugliest feeling I can positively I.D.

KARL: Yer a bad sport?

MITCHELL: I can't even play a board game without feeling it!

KARL: The Boy Scouts fuckin' ruined you, ya know that?

MITCHELL: However you care to marginalize it.

KARL: What are you so afraid of?

MITCHELL: I'm not afraid.

KARL: That I'll what...annihilate you if you...

MITCHELL: No.

KARL: ...engage with me now...

MITCHELL: *Engage?*

KARL: ...in a real way?

MITCHELL: Bingo!

KARL: *(Beat.)* Pardon?

MITCHELL: Aggressive, provocative behavior has got nothing to do with...

KARL: Aggressive?

MITCHELL: ...with being *real.* It's a trick—stirring things up, creating conflict, to give the delusional the illusion that real honesty is going on— it's a trick!

KARL: *(Beat.)* I'm sorry, you've momentarily dazed me.

MITCHELL: I'm saying that you feel real when creating some conflict, 'cause you thrive on competition and you need to win!

KARL: Because guys do that.

MITCHELL: Because...

KARL: I wanna get you in the sandbox is what yer saying.

MITCHELL: It's a sickness inside me!

KARL: And this is exclusively a male phenomenon? Aside from like... Margaret Thatcher or maybe Madonna?

MITCHELL: I just always liked girls.

KARL: Of course.

MITCHELL: No. I mean *always*. Like from the crib. Like from birth.

KARL: Uh-huh.

MITCHELL: And I came early of the opinion that girls, at least, wouldn't beat the crap out of me constantly.

KARL: How wrong you were.

MITCHELL: I wanted all my friends to be girls. Being with them was intoxicating. I'm not talking about sex.

KARL: Okay.

MITCHELL: I'm talking about feeling not competitive, but honest. And emotional. And unreserved and expansive. Like all of me being in use at once!

KARL: Who are these women?

MITCHELL: What?

KARL: I'd like to meet one.

MITCHELL: Shut up.

KARL: You idealize the shit outta them. Like literally. Like they don't pinch the daily loaf.

MITCHELL: Must you…

KARL: And you gotta be outta yer tree, if you don't think the whole is competitive!

MITCHELL: That's my experience.

KARL: That is romanticism, man.

MITCHELL: I'm just not afraid to…

KARL: What?

MITCHELL: Tell me something.

KARL: Yeah?

MITCHELL: What about Malerie?

KARL: What about her?

MITCHELL: "She's not my girlfriend."

KARL: What?

MITCHELL: That what yer always sayin'.

KARL: I am?

MITCHELL: Yeah, for years you've been sayin' it.

KARL: Okay! Well, fine. That's probably because I have a different idea of being with a woman than you do.

MITCHELL: Obviously.

KARL: Listen to me. It *is* a competition. You come over and play a nice game of *Sorry!* with me. I'll kick yer ass and maybe you'll sulk for an hour.

Later you'll have a beer with me and we'll get on with it. The whole process will take about ninety minutes.

MITCHELL: You never...

KARL: But some of these *girls* you've had are still bangin' around inside you like ghosts, 'cause you played *their* shit. I mean, get out the holy water, man!

MITCHELL: Maybe. But it's not...

KARL: Don't get me wrong—it's not for lack of trying. And I can't figure out where you get it from...

MITCHELL: What?

KARL: This faith.

MITCHELL: This...?

KARL: *Faith,* yes, everytime that this next one, is *really* it. You produce this faith like some perennial plant in the earth. Like photosynthesis. It never ceases to astonish me. I maybe had that like *once.* And I'm *never* gonna get it back.

MITCHELL: Who's to say...?

KARL: You can go places that I can't go, Mitchell. It's deeply human, a little scary, and I'm envious, ya know? But there are things that I know you need with a woman that you will never get until you let them fucking have it!

MITCHELL: I'm not sure I believe that.

KARL: You are seriously visually-impaired, if you can't see that the most darkly primal competition is going on in any relationship between the two sexes. Maybe for gays, too. But I can't speak to that.

MITCHELL: Whaddya talkin'?

KARL: It's like nothing less than a fight to the death, and you gotta get over yer aversion and throw on some armor if yer gonna sally forth into this shit, again.

MITCHELL: Don't get all...

KARL: What?

MITCHELL: ...medieval on me.

KARL: Well, that's what it is, Mitchell. It's like the fuckin' Crusades. Someone is trying to bend the other to some unspoken or overspoken even standard of what is right and true, and the other one winds up being an occupied territory.

MITCHELL: You are one cynical fuck.

KARL: I can't believe yer runnin' around out in the world not knowing this. *(Karl drains his beer, crushes the can, and flips it over his shoulder.)*

MITCHELL: Does this go for everybody?

KARL: Yeah, pretty much. And what I'm tellin' ya...it's not, okay, that I don't *like* women. I do. A lot. I just don't think of them as little flowers. I mean, why should they be? They're fighting for their lives.

MITCHELL: *(Beat.) Does this go for everybody?*

KARL: Didn't I just say?

MITCHELL: Does this go for, say...yer mom?

KARL: My mom? Yeah, sure.

MITCHELL: She knows you think of her this way?

KARL: I don't think of *her* that way.

MITCHELL: So, there's exceptions?

KARL: Not really. She's my *mom*. Like the woman I see every Friday afternoon at Allied Irish is my *bank teller*. I don't have that kind of relationship with them. They go home and mix it up with their *husbands*. We never get into the ring.

MITCHELL: I see.

KARL: Ya do?

MITCHELL: Of course. I see now.

KARL: What?

MITCHELL: Of course Malerie's not yer girlfriend...

KARL: What is yer fascination today...?

MITCHELL: Yer disabled.

KARL: I'm...?!

MITCHELL: You need like wheelchair access into it.

KARL: I'm just...I try to be realistic.

MITCHELL: That's very orderly of you.

KARL: You don't wanna hear about it...

MITCHELL: *I* don't?!

KARL: 's right in fronna ya, tho'.

MITCHELL: Is it?

KARL: *(Muttering.)* You think about yer mom...

MITCHELL: What?

KARL: Yeah! Yeah! You think about *yer* mom!

MITCHELL: This is not going to work.

KARL: Why does a man, like Stan The Man, keel over of a coronary at the age of fifty-three?

MITCHELL: Bad food, no exercise, and a stubborn refusal to take his blood-pressure medicine?

KARL: He was a casualty, man, of this very conflict we're talkin'. How long were they married—yer folks?

MITCHELL: Nineteen years.

KARL: Nineteen *years*. And then the split.

MITCHELL: Yeah.

KARL: And how did he age, Mitchell?

MITCHELL: Uh...

KARL: Huh?

MITCHELL: He...fast. He...

KARL: Right?

MITCHELL: Yer right. He got old fast.

KARL: And yer mom and...

MITCHELL: Horace.

KARL: Got hitched...

MITCHELL: ...right away. Yeah. They did.

KARL: That's a blow.

MITCHELL: It did take him out. The break-up.

KARL: Yeah.

MITCHELL: He just disappeared for about four months at first, ya know? And the next time I saw him he was just a different guy. He didn't ever really recover. He...

KARL: So...

MITCHELL: God! I can't believe I never really...

KARL: What?

MITCHELL: Put it together. I guess...

KARL: Ya just didn't want to.

MITCHELL: What?

KARL: ...*consider* it. It might mean that you'd hate her.

MITCHELL: My mom?

KARL: Yeah. And that's harsh.

MITCHELL: Like she killed him?

KARL: You know she *didn't*...

MITCHELL: But it feels...

KARL: ...like she did, yeah. It's a big deal. And it's not like something you could probably ever...I don't know if I could ever ask my mom.

MITCHELL: Maybe you should.

KARL: Yeah, well...you think I don't wanna?

MITCHELL: Right.

KARL: There was probably even a time—like once—maybe when I coulda. But now…I give. I give up. I'm on my own. It's…Christ!

MITCHELL: What?

KARL: Such a waste! Just…it's Ed, ya know? Right there. My failure with him is like the whole thing in a nutshell. My "family"! I…

MITCHELL: Yeah?

KARL: When Pop died and I got there, when I got home, my whole family was just so different for once. Like all the little lies got suspended for the duration. For that one week.

MITCHELL: Yeah.

KARL: Everybody stopped hiding themselves so hard and I really finally felt for once that I belonged to something there. That we… *(Beat.)* I never told you this before, but it's key. It's why I know, okay? It's why I know I gotta…

MITCHELL: What?

KARL: The last night before the service, during the, you know, visiting hours…

MITCHELL: Viewing…

KARL: At the funeral home, right. It's late. Everyone's left. The mortician, or whatever tells me it's *past* time to go—kinda all put-out, the dick—and sashays away. Me and Ed are left. We're alone for the first time since we got home.

MITCHELL: Uh-huh.

KARL: I walk over to him and he just like collapses in my arms! He almost knocks me over. And he's sobbin', standin' there in his uniform and all. He's hangin' on to me and just heaving, weeping, for a long time. Like a coupla minutes. And then, it's over. He…he can't even *look* at me! I know he maybe feels weird. So, I start to say something. He just…he walks out of the room. He never says anything.

MITCHELL: People can't always handle…

KARL: I know that! But never? Ever? Say anything? And it's not like I didn't try…try to get it back with him. But it's only ever gotten worse since. Like it was some mistake or…

MITCHELL: Ya think…?

KARL: It's just that there's nothing I've ever experienced, ever, with anyone, aside from you, as intimate and real as what it was to grieve and get through that time together.

MITCHELL: I know.

KARL: And then to see it evaporate! That the bitterness, and the bullshit games, and all the lousy fucking denial could resume after we'd been through all that! That it could be so willfully forgotten! It was our finest hour and our final chance, probably, to really change!

MITCHELL: You'll...

KARL: And that's why I come here. That's why I remember and why I push you. 'Cause I want it to mean something!

MITCHELL: It...

KARL: I want it to be real!

MITCHELL: It is.

KARL: It's not an easy place to get...for me to get to with just anyone...

MITCHELL: I know...

KARL: But you bring it out in me, ya bastard! And you can't...

MITCHELL: I won't!

KARL: ...just cut-out! It's not casual! I...

MITCHELL: It's...

KARL: I need you to hang in and not hide. I swear...

MITCHELL: I'm...I'm...

KARL: I won't recover again from that kinda betrayal!

MITCHELL: I'm goin'...!

(At this moment Mitchell begins to tremble, his eyes roll back, he topples over and hits his head.)

KARL: Shit!

(Karl grabs Mitchell and holds him, supporting his weight with his body. They stand together uneasily.)

KARL: Mitch?

MITCHELL: *(Faintly.)* Yeah?

KARL: Where are you?

MITCHELL: Neither...

KARL: Huh?

MITCHELL: Neither here nor there.

KARL: *(Beat.)* Couldya be more specific?

MITCHELL: *(In a loud voice.)* Whaddya tryin' to do? Make a jerk outta yerself?!

KARL: Who's that?

MITCHELL: It's a perfectly good pair! Now, get the hell outta here!

KARL: Mitchell? Are you there at all? Mitch?

MITCHELL: (Faintly.) I'm gettin...

KARL: Somethin' angry, I know. Let's shift ground.

(Karl drags Mitchell across the grave toward a bench. Just as they arrive

Mitchell falls to the ground, Karl above him. Mitchell grabs Karl urgently, speaking the following in Russian.)

MITCHELL: "She said the very thing. She said the very thing. And I was twice wronged. Twice wronged, my son!"

(Mitchell falls silent and limp. After a moment, Mitchell begins to speak in his father's voice—a flat mid-western tenor.)

MITCHELL/STAN: Karl?

KARL: Uh…yeah?

MITCHELL/STAN: Stan Hill.

KARL: Mr. Hill?!?

MITCHELL/STAN: Stan. Call me Stan, Karl. How is he?

KARL: Mitchell?

MITCHELL/STAN: My son, yes. How is he?

KARL: Ya know…not great, Stan. He's not.

MITCHELL/STAN: Well, it only gets harder.

KARL: Huh? Whaddya mean?!

MITCHELL/STAN: I can say no more.

KARL: You haven't said anything!

MITCHELL/STAN: Karl?

KARL: Yeah?

MITCHELL/STAN: Not to be complaining or whathaveyou—I'm glad you boys remember us

KARL: How is Pop?

MITCHELL/STAN: He's dead. Ya know? How should he be?

KARL: Right. Sorry.

MITCHELL/STAN: Forget it. Karl?

KARL: Yeah?

MITCHELL/STAN: We want you, yer father and I…oh!

KARL: What?

MITCHELL/STAN: He likes that gal of yers.

KARL: Mal?

MITCHELL/STAN: Who else?

KARL: Pop likes Mal?

MITCHELL/STAN: Yup. Likes her teeth.

KARL: Her *teeth?*

MITCHELL/STAN: Apparently, yes. We didn't dwell.

KARL: Her teeth…

MITCHELL/STAN: We want you boys to get on with it. We're glad you found each other, that yer friends. We're proud of you. But we want you to get on with it.

KARL: We'll do our best.

MITCHELL/STAN: What *can* you do?

KARL: Right.

MITCHELL/STAN: And Mitchell…

KARL: Yeah?

MITCHELL/STAN: He worries too much. Just like his grandfather.

KARL: That's what I tell him.

MITCHELL/STAN: Good. Tell him some more.

KARL: Okay.

MITCHELL/STAN: And another thing…

KARL: Yeah?

MITCHELL/STAN: Mitchell shouldn't be too hard on Fran.

KARL: Fran?

MITCHELL/STAN: His mother.

KARL: Oh.

MITCHELL/STAN: You don't know her name? I thought you were his friend.

KARL: It's never come up.

MITCHELL/STAN: Whatever. He shouldn't be too hard on her. People make choices. Sometimes they're not too thoughtful.

KARL: We're only human.

MITCHELL/STAN: Speak for yerself!

KARL: Sorry.

MITCHELL/STAN: Forget it. What I'm saying, Karl, is…ya hafta let go. Things happen when they're supposed to. Mitchell needs to know this. I wish I was around to tell him.

KARL: So does he.

MITCHELL/STAN: Yeah, well…I try not to be bitter.

KARL: Uh-huh.

MITCHELL/STAN: Never did a body any good.

KARL: Right.

MITCHELL/STAN: Now, I gotta run.

KARL: Wait!

MITCHELL/STAN: I'm sorry it hadta be so brief, but, ya know…business!

KARL: What kind of…?

MITCHELL/STAN: I can say no more.

KARL: Ya haven't said…

(Suddenly Mitchell clutches his left arm in pain.)

MITCHELL: Ow! Fuck!

KARL: What?

MITCHELL: Shit! Like someone just kicked me in the...

KARL: You okay?

MITCHELL: Fuck!

KARL: Take it easy.

MITCHELL: Man.

KARL: Just breathe.

MITCHELL: Man.

KARL: Ya alright?

MITCHELL: Yeah, I'm...I dunno. I'm okay. *(Beat.)* Whaddid...?

KARL: It's foreign language day.

MITCHELL: Huh?

KARL: Some Russian it sounded like.

MITCHELL: Huh.

KARL: And yer father.

MITCHELL: Dad? How...how was he?

KARL: Kinda cranky, actually.

MITCHELL: I've...I've never...

KARL: I know.

MITCHELL: Whaddid?

KARL: I think the gist of it is, he wants you to sorta not get too hung up on the past. But just to kinda take a breath and know that stuff will come to ya.

MITCHELL: Good stuff?

KARL: Well, like I said—he wasn't real upbeat. But, yeah, I think he wants ya to be hopeful, at least.

MITCHELL: Wow. *(Beat.)* Okay.

KARL: Yeah. *(Beat.)* Alright?

MITCHELL: Let's do it.

(Karl hands Mitchell the flask. They both drink.)

MITCHELL: To 'em.

KARL: The Da's.

MITCHELL: There's not much left.

KARL: I know.

MITCHELL: Maybe we should dilute it with somethin' fine so a little of the remains remain.

KARL: Maybe. Maybe we don't do this anymore.

MITCHELL: Whaddya mean?

KARL: Like next year, I mean. Maybe it's enough if we know...

MITCHELL: Know what?

KARL: I'm gettin' married, Mitchell.

MITCHELL: What?

KARL: Gettin' hitched.

MITCHELL: To...to Malerie?

KARL: To Mal, yeah. What the fuck.

MITCHELL: What the...

KARL: I meant to tell you this.

MITCHELL: And now seemed a convenient time.

KARL: More or less.

MITCHELL: Swell.

KARL: What?

MITCHELL: What what?

KARL: What's the matter?

MITCHELL: Nothin'.

KARL: Why are gettin' all weird now I told ya?

MITCHELL: Forget it.

KARL: What? Yer mad at me?

MITCHELL: Yeah, whaddya think?

KARL: I dunno. *Why* are you mad at me?

MITCHELL: Because it's just so...

KARL: What?

MITCHELL: ...easy for you!

KARL: That is...

MITCHELL: So easy...

KARL: ...not true!

MITCHELL: You just control the whole board! The whole fucking game! While I'd just give like anything if...if...

KARL: What?

MITCHELL: If someone, anyone, who I lose my heart to would weigh the pre-ponderance of evidence—like my complete devotion against whatever the always impossible to articulate so-called "problem" is, that won't let her stay for pancakes with an option on forever! And then *you...you,* who could basically give a shit—yer gettin' it! What I'd saw my leg off and pull my liver out for! So, congratulations, Karl! I hope you'll be very happy!

KARL: Thanks. Could I get that in writing? I think Hallmark might be inter-ested.

MITCHELL: Fuck!

KARL: Don't you know...?

MITCHELL: I don't know anything!

KARL: That is such bullshit!

MITCHELL: Why would you...?

KARL: What?

MITCHELL: Why are you gettin' married?

KARL: 'Cause I'm not...I'm not gonna do any better.

MITCHELL: That's terrific.

KARL: I...

MITCHELL: Maybe ya oughta work that into yer vows somewhere.

KARL: It's not gonna happen for me, Mitchell. I didn't really believe that it *existed*, even, until...

MITCHELL: What? What?!

KARL: What I need right now, Mitchell, more than yer curses, is a little of yer famous faith. I need that now.

MITCHELL: I'm sorry. I just...

KARL: Mitchell, I probably am impaired.

MITCHELL: Disabled.

KARL: I probably am. And that scares me. Because if I am, I might could screw-up real bad. And I won't be able to forgive myself if I ever really hurt Mal.

MITCHELL: You won't be the only one.

KARL: It's not easy! It's not easy for me at all, Mitchell! I thought I had all this worked out. I don't.

MITCHELL: Yeah.

KARL: I know that, I do. But I need...if I'm gonna go through with this I'm gonna need you.

MITCHELL: Why me?

KARL: You stubborn...

MITCHELL: I'm askin'...

KARL: ...fuck!

MITCHELL: ...'cause you gotta know that I can't—no one can help you with this thing if you don't give over the guerrilla-warfare approach...

KARL: What?

MITCHELL: ...to romance. Shut up.

KARL: I...

MITCHELL: You gotta loosen the vice-grips and really take a chance.

KARL: I want to.

MITCHELL: And there are no guarantees, ya know. That's the catch. You can't get it right unless yer really open—it won't mean anything. But once yer there, anything goes. She could discard you like totally carelessly. But it's the risk you take.

KARL: I'm gonna try.

MITCHELL: Good.

KARL: What else?

MITCHELL: That's all I know.

KARL: C'mon!

MITCHELL: What?

KARL: That's not enough!

MITCHELL: Sorry.

KARL: I need...

MITCHELL: What?

KARL: It's not all down to me. And *you* gotta know this...

MITCHELL: What?

KARL: That it's not all down to yer wife, yer lover, or yer shrink to connect the dots either. Like ya get it all through sex or psychotherapy just 'cause everybody tells ya so.

MITCHELL: Zeitgeist.

KARL: Huh?

MITCHELL: That's what they call that.

KARL: *(Beat.)* Shut the fuck up.

MITCHELL: Sorry.

KARL: What I thought I'd have with my father as a man didn't happen. He's gone. Pop. And Ed? Maybe he'll come around someday. I doubt it. And how long do I hafta wait? I need you in a way no one else can help me. Not Malerie. Not just me on my own. Not anyone! I mean it!

MITCHELL: Karl...

KARL: I need my family around my now. And you are the family I got, Mitchell. I need you to sign on to this and take it serious.

MITCHELL: Karl...

KARL: You can't go now! The good brother I never had, who understood, and let me grieve, and not be the tough guy all the time!

MITCHELL: I won't. I promise.

KARL: I just...

MITCHELL: I promise.

KARL: It's not unselfish. I have a serious need to keep you on the planet. I think if you weren't, it'd sorta be like if the miracle force of gravity disappeared, ya know? Just up and skawkered. I'd probably just start floating uncontrollably upward and no one would even notice until I burst into flames exiting the earth's atmosphere...

MITCHELL: ...charred bits and ash falling back scattered debris...

KARL: ...all over Florida. *(Beat.)* s'cold.

MITCHELL: Yer just now noticing?

KARL: You wanna get out?

MITCHELL: Sure.

KARL: Mitch?

MITCHELL: Yeah?

KARL: Try not to worry so much.

MITCHELL: I'll try.

KARL: Good.

MITCHELL: Runs in the family, though.

(Karl hands him the flask. Mitchell un-caps it, thinking. He hands it back.)

MITCHELL: Kill it.

KARL: Huh?

MITCHELL: My brother.

(Karl takes the flask, gestures skyward and begins to drink. Lights fade.)

THE END